the

Wonderful Wideness *of* Being

Jantine Brinkman

The Wonderful Wideness of Being
Jantine Brinkman
ISBN 978-1-77342-036-3

Produced by IndieBookLauncher.com
www.IndieBookLauncher.com
Cover Photography: Tracy Marshall
Cover Design: Saul Bottcher
Interior Design and Typesetting: Saul Bottcher

The body text of this book is set in Adobe Caslon.

Notice of Rights
All text copyright 2017 Jantine Brinkman, all rights reserved.

Also Available
EPUB edition, ISBN 978-1-77342-037-0
Kindle edition, ISBN 978-1-77342-038-7

CONTENTS

Foreword 7
1. Setting the stage 9
2. Beliefs and statistics 17
3. About origin 25
4. Our blueprint 31
5. Consciousness adventures 37
6. Out-of-body 45
7. Essence essentials 51
8. The creation of a focus 63
9. Me, my selves and I 75
10. Probables 83
11. Dimensions 91
12. Shifting 101
13. Transition 111
    Afterword 127
    References 129
    About the Author 131

Acknowledgments

A big Thank You with much appreciation:

To my mother and my brother for their support and care.

To Tracy, Jan, Debbie, Oba, Marij, Arthur, Francie and Michele for their support and inspiration.

To Tracy for letting me use one of her amazing photographs for the cover of this book.

To Francisco, Ulrike and Trudy for their support.

To Mary, Tara and Nuno for the Elias, Tompkin and Lawrence sessions, and for their support to this book.

And last but not least to Elias, Tompkin and Lawrence for lending their tremendous and supportive energy.

Foreword

Once upon a time there was no time. Consciousness families, each with their particular focus and interests, created our universe and the notion of time to allow for physical experiences by physical forms. No gods or Abrahamic entities were involved here, nor was Darwinist evolution. Conscious energies brought our world into existence. Energies that are us, no hierarchy, no external forces. Us creating ourselves in the wideness and complexity of consciousness.

I am flabbergasted and pleased when I discover this on the Elias Web site, and I want to know more. From my visits to the Elias Facebook Forum I already know that Elias is a discarnate entity, or more accurately an essence, channeled by Mary Ennis since 1995. I notice that the web site is up to date and contains a large amount of transcripts and audios of the sessions that Elias has with clients, via Mary.

I am impressed by the detailedness and the extensiveness of the transcript material on consciousness, its forms, its creation process, and much more. Rather quickly I decide to dedicate a study to the wideness of individual consciousness, and use this material for it. The session transcripts are all numbered, which makes it easy for me to refer to them, and easy for you to find them on the web site, at *www.eliasweb.org*.

Mainstream philosophy and psychology books I have already excluded completely when I make that decision. They still provide little quality information on the topic of the wideness of individual awareness, because they almost automatically exclude the notion of the existence of consciousness outside the physical brain and body. Apparently nothing has changed in those academic areas since I wrote my first book, a comparative literature study on free will after life, which was published in 2013.

Although I highly value the Seth books, I have decided to not use them as the main source material for my book. One reason for that is the age factor. Elias is a 21st century source, Seth came through in the second half of the 20th century and at that time the general mindset was significantly different from the one that is currently predominant, in my opinion.

The primary ground for my choice for Elias, however, is the detailedness of his communications on consciousness topics. To expand the bandwidth of his material I have inserted transcript excerpts from my own sessions with him and with the essences of Tompkin, whose sessions are available at *www.tompkin.info*, and Lawrence, who are both closely related to Elias as you will find.

In addition to this I have added some of my dreams and out-of-body experiences to this book. They have enhanced my quest for the wideness of individual consciousness, and they serve to illustrate some of the presented concepts.

In summary, the book is the narrative of my personal journey through internal and external materials. The chapters contain quite a bit of basic Elias concepts. Your head may start spinning while reading about them, especially in the first chapters; once you have internalized their content the later chapters will be easier to grasp.

I wish you a marvelous and enchanting reading experience.

1
Setting the stage

I close and put away the Seth book on the nature of personal reality that I am reading for the third time now. I am done studying topics while sitting in the ivory tower of my home. I sit down at my desk and open Google to search for a community that focuses on consciousness topics. I want to meet new people, preferably knowledgeable on the material that I enjoy. Like-minded folks. The search results appear quickly on my screen after typing the key words. I notice a link to a Seth Facebook page and activate it. The page asks me to request for access, which is granted quickly. A whole new world opens up to me. In the following days I read lots of quotes from the books, as well as the reactions to these quotes. When triggered I add my five cents to the comment section, and in general I enjoy myself with the subsequent reactions. I get to know a few members a bit better. One of them, Steve, tells me that I should check out the Elias Facebook Forum. He is rather explicit in his preference for Elias, and I become curious. After gaining access to that page as well, I open it and start reading.

Statistics? What on earth are the members talking about?, I am thinking while reading a few posts. They mention families, orientations, focuses, and what have you. I feel totally clueless on my first trips through the forum. I don't want to ask the moderator anything about the content, but I am determined to find out what all these terms mean, especially as they are used so frequently. Luckily Steve has given me the web address of the Elias forum web site. In his communications to me he is very positive about the quality of the information on that site. I scroll through its homepage, then go to the introduction. The first page to catch my attention is about how it all started. What a shock it must have been for the spectators to see Mary's energy being 'taken over' by another energy that could talk through her! It was April 1995 when that initial session took place, and it was not planned. The little group who witnessed it knew very well about Seth appearing through Jane Roberts, but they did not expect to see that happen through their friend.

I enjoy reading about unusual events and want to know more. My next stop is the digest section. I quickly end up in the overview page of the essence families.

The term essence I put aside for investigation later on. First the families. I scroll down to the first snippet. "There are nine families of consciousness which are connected with this particular physical dimension, which in conjunction with yourselves are creating of this particular reality and orchestrate the manifestation of this particular dimension", Elias says in session 270.

I have to read that sentence three or four times to understand at least a bit of the info. So the consciousness families create the universe, interesting! Something to keep in mind. I start to look for the names and characteristics of these families. The essence families that are mentioned on that same page, are Sumafi, Milumet, Gramada, Vold, Ilda, Sumari, Tumold, Zuli and Borledim. So, who are they?

Elias says, amongst other things, the following about the Sumafi family in session 67: "[…] this family incorporates the focus of teaching. It incorporates teachers of every element and every subject of your existence. […] In other time periods within your history, they have been 'keepers of knowledge.' They have manifest as scribes. Many have chosen religious-focuses. They are quite intent upon keeping truths. Their intent also is in the direction of the least distortion. Therefore, within any element of teaching, they strive to incorporate the least distortion, the most original, the most pure."

Teaching. Not my hobby. A least distortion scribe, that works fine. I ponder upon the information for a while, and then, in the same session, I notice a piece about their playfulness which attracts me greatly: "These essences also, of Sumafi, I will express, are playful. They do not incorporate the seriousness that you think of, within physical focus, of 'solemn teachers!' [...] They are also quite experiential, understanding the value of experience with teaching. You learn through experience; therefore they are quite directing of experiences, and hold much desire to be experiencing."

That's more like it! Playfulness and learning through experience. I can relate to that.

Enthusiastically, still reading the transcript of session 67, I move on to the description of the the Sumari family: "The Sumari are playful. They are creative. They are spiritual. They are your artists. They are not teachers of art; they are doers. [...] This essence family incorporates great creativity."

Cool family! My eyes open up wider when I also read: "They are not introverted or shy individuals! They are quite extroverted. They also are quite independent. They do not align themselves with groups. They do not align themselves with societies or governments or religions. They are your rebellious group. [...] They do not conform. You will find, in movements of cultures, individuals who are refusing to conform to the norm. These individuals belong to the Sumari."

That is me!! Oh dear, now what? Do I belong to the Sumafi or the Sumari family? I am lost.

I quickly scroll through the sections of the other families, but find little that I personally recognize in them. The Tumolds "are the healers", an excellent focus in my opinion, which is not too far away from me, but not my first priority; the Zuli family "relates to physical expression"; that is definitely not me but a very useful priority in this physical universe.

The Borledims "primary focus is to be creating of new individuals", that can't be me either. Luckily others are related to this family, otherwise I might not have come to existence.

The Ilda "[…] focus is exchange. They are travelers. They may be manifest as merchants, as gypsies, as seamen; any individuals that travel and exchange ideas of cultures. They are the 'mixers.'" Nice! But not me, although I love to travel.

The Vold family "would be focused upon by you as being reformers. They are not interested in the status quo. They change themselves, they change where their location is, they change elements around them […] they change your world! […] They also are very, very emotional." That is a definite 'no' with regards to my not so emotional personality. Interesting family though.

The individuals of the Gramada family "are the ones responsible for establishment of your societies, your governments, your institutions, your religions. Others 'take up' the work and establishment of these elements, but this family projects the original; the idea; the concept; the information." I much value their existence, but establishing societies and so forth is not what I do.

Last but not least, on the Milumets, in that same session 67: "This family incorporates the focus of spiritualists, mystics. They manifest mainly within what you will view as primitives. […] These individuals are very connected with nature. They hold an extraordinary connection with creatures. It is quite easy for these individuals to exchange telepathically, and also empathically, with creatures, and with all elements of nature." Wonderful connection creations, but not my primary focus.

¶

Now that I have a basic insight in the families, I want to know about their members, the essences. I have noticed in the forum that references are made to an additional web site, the Elias Web, and I google it. To my relief I discover that this web site is up to date. An enormous amount of material is available on essences on that web site, I find out while using its search function. I notice that I need to look into the general topic of consciousness before going into essence information. Consciousness is the base of the entire universe and of all other dimensions, physical and non-physical. Consciousness is energy, and as you may remember from physics class, energy cannot be separated nor destroyed. That means there is no separation between elements of consciousness. An individual is not separated from another in consciousness, just in (body) form. As Elias summarizes in session 132: "The commonality of consciousness is self-awareness. […] A molecule of air is aware of itself, and its existence, and its function. You, in your highly developed state, are aware of your existence and of your functioning. You are the same. […] All, underline all, consciousness is connected with all consciousness. Energy may not be separated. It is."

Consciousness was already present before our known universe was created. Before essences came into existence, Elias says "there were elements of consciousness. You may also term these to be "units", which others have expressed previously. These elements of consciousness know no limits of time or space. You may think of these as very tiny, black holes. You may think of them, if you will, in physical terms, as elements smaller than your smallest physical particles; but these elements are that which creates all physical expression. Everything, within every universe, within every dimension, is created by these elements of consciousness; and they are everything. They are not only the driving force behind matter and action, but are matter and action also; this being the basis of what you term to be 'god'". (Session 79)

More basic than this it can't get. Now, what is an essence? From the same session: "Essence is what we will term a portion of this encompassing whole, although not a portion! [...] Your intent and function is to incorporate intellect and intuition, to be directing of your universe as you have created it. Therefore, make no mistake; you direct all of your physical manifestation, in every area."

Essence "is the personality identification, in individuality, of consciousness", Elias states in session 191a. Also known as the soul in Christianity and some esoteric traditions. As essences we create. From the same session: "There have been essences in groups, which we identify as families, that are directly connected to the creation of this dimension and physical reality in its entirety—your entire known universe. This is only one universe, which occupies the same space arrangement as all other universes. You are merely aware of this one. There have been, as has been expressed, essences creating this planet and planetary system, which have been identified in relation to the Seers." To be clear, the Seers are the members of the Sumafi family mentioned in the previous section.

In short, an essence is an individualized element of consciousness. It belongs to a family of its own choice. And it interacts with other essences all the time: "Let me express to you also, essences are continuously in motion and engaging actions of mergence with other essences, and as this action occurs, many times there are actions created that initiate fragmentation, and as these essences merge together, the fragmenting essence may be a combination of qualities and tones of those essences which are within mergence." (Session 504)

Every essence holds its tone, which can be translated into a name, but it can change tone when it wants to. And every essence holds its own characteristics. As you remember there is no separation, nor between an essence and its incarnations.

Some essences love to investigate. Other essences may have artistic or an athletic inclinations. All essences love to explore. This is more or less their raison d'être. There is much more to say about essences than I have mentioned above, but I will discuss that later on in this book.

2
Beliefs and statistics

It takes me some time to digest the material about consciousness, essences and families. Meanwhile, in day to day life I am consuming my savings as I do not have a job. I don't like the sense of diminishing funds too much, so I decide to dedicate a few months to winning the jackpot in a large national or European lottery. Nobody can accuse me of not being ambitious.

I am reading various books with for this purpose. They all mention exercises on investigating your beliefs when it comes to attracting funds. So, what is it that I believe about money that isn't functioning, I ask myself.

I jump into the pool of my lightest and darkest beliefs around the money subject. I meditate, repeat affirmations, sit still, and relax my physical, emotional and mental bodies. I do everything by the books. I notice various beliefs, such as 'I don't deserve to have much money'; 'money is the root of all evil'; 'money will soon disappear as an exchange unit anyway'; 'I have to do work to get and deserve money', etcetera. I recognize acknowledge and accept them when encountered, but I still do not have a few million euros on my bank account. Why not? What am I doing wrong? I go to the Elias web site again, and discover in session 1158 that apparently it is a matter of me wanting it too much:

"Many individuals express that they want to be winning, and for the most part the individuals that actually accomplish that are not focusing their energy in that direction very intensely. This is the reason that they generate such genuine surprise in their accomplishment. For the action was to play the game, not necessarily to win, which is quite a different motivation. This is a reflection of all of your reality, my friend. In your terms, physically, you win in the moments in which you are merely allowing yourself to play rather than focusing intensely upon the action of winning, for the outcome is generated in the moment."

As if that isn't confronting me enough with my inability to win, I then come across the notion of 'lack'. Focusing upon my lack of money as a motivation to play the lottery, I will not win anyway. On the contrary, as stated in session 3147, "If you are paying attention to what you do not have, you will create more lack." I start to laugh out loud. It is obviously time for a different attitude from my side. Einstein knew that a 100 years ago when he gave his definition of insanity: doing the same thing over and over again and expecting different results.

I have to go back to basics, is my impression. One of the first things that parents teach their children is that they will be fine. Pain will pass. The child will feel better soon. I can work with that. The core trick is to realize that I am safe right now, I am not living in a war zone, I have a roof over my head and I have food and drinks. As Elias confirms, "Trust is the lack of doubt and the knowing that you can and that you already have. That is what trust is." (Session 2227)

I want that trust, and a good life in which I follow my priorities and interests. To thrive and be trusting seems perfect to me, and I find a nice snippet on the 'how to' that I want to share here: "In paying attention to you, in genuinely—genuinely—turning your attention to you, not generating or concerning yourself with comparisons, not projecting your attention outwardly to other individuals or even to situations and circumstances, but turning your attention to you and allowing yourself to examine the influences of the beliefs that you hold upon your perception. Once recognizing what influences your perception, you may also recognize how this becomes an obstacle or how this restricts your choices. And thusly in acknowledgment of these beliefs, you may also allow yourself the freedom of choice, which in itself shall begin to generate more of an expression of trust within you." (Session 1070)

That statement I can buy into easily, as I know from experience that turning my attention inwardly has led me to terminate an undesired counseling path, followed by an immediate start of an heart-felt investigation into the wideness of our awareness. Exploring and focusing on what you want to do deep down, and actually doing that, is the best way towards a fulfilling life, I discover. Winning the lottery is no longer a priority in my life; not that I would be opposed to hitting the jackpot though.

ʃ

I have been enjoying my visits to the Elias Facebook forum tremendously since I joined. So much high quality information that is new to me is shared there; I love that. I have gotten to know more and more forum members, and some offer me to ask Elias about my statistics. They involve amongst others the family my essence belongs to and the one that my focus aligns with. What is a focus anyway? It is an individualized life. I am a focus of and created by my essence in this lifetime. And I am also essence; again, no separation.

The main characteristic of a focus is movement, as becomes clear from this snippet from session 69: "Think for a moment of yourself as being a motion. Think of yourself as an action; not as the particle, but as the wave, the motion, continuing within a particular direction. Now think of yourself as the whole of your essence. This individual focus is a motion. You, within essence, move in all directions, simultaneously, continuously. Each focus, each facet of your essence moves in one direction.

Therefore you, within this physical focus, are one movement of your essence. Within this, each movement incorporates its individuality. A forward direction is not a sideways direction. Therefore, each direction incorporates its own individuality, its own identity, its own impression within essence; but it is one direction within all directions."

I continue my search, and find another and very intriguing snippet on focuses, this time in session 80: "[…] each lifetime, as you term this, is a focus. It is a focus of essence, and occurs simultaneously to all other focuses. Therefore, all of which you term to be past lives are individual focuses of your essence, viewing and experiencing physical development."

I hold my horses. Simultaneous occurrence of all of the focuses of my essence? No linearity here? No time? The theories of reincarnation, one life after another, seem instantly invalid. Oh dear. That is just so different from what I have assumed to be true so far.

From my initial research I assume that my essence belongs to either the Sumafi or Sumari consciousness family. As a focus you usually belong to the same family as your essence does, but not necessarily, and in addition as Elias says, "you hold alignments, characteristics, leanings, towards other essence families. You are, within your focus, involved or aligned with two essence families; this meaning you are grouped with two simultaneously. Therefore, you incorporate the actions and the focus of both. You may hold characteristics of other essence families also. You will find that you hold elements of all of these essence families. The particular essence families that you align to, you "hold yourself" as a "family member". Therefore you belong, simultaneously, to two families." (Session 102)

That is interesting to read. So I may well have connections with both the Sumafi and Sumari families, and maybe others.

There are more statistics that catch my eye. Orientation is one of them. What is orientation? Elias gives a clear definition of that in session 378: "Orientation is your perception: how you view yourselves, how you view your world, how you interact with yourself, how you interact with all other individuals, how you interact with your environment. It is the most influencing element which creates your perception. Your perception creates your reality. In this, there are three orientations of perception."

These are: soft, intermediate and common, I notice while reading on. In summary, individuals with a common orientation are interested in activities and creations outside themselves. They project their inner self outwardly, in physical elements. Those with an intermediate orientation create inwardly. They perceive more with their inner senses, the intuition. Their attention is on emotions. The soft oriented are focused upon interaction and involvement. Their expression can be outwardly or inwardly; that is not really important to them. They may interact and be involved in people or nature or what have you.

Common and soft do not strike a chord with me. I decide to dive deeper into the intermediates and stumble upon this statement from session 201205031: "Whatever you do, it is more important to do it effectively or do it more efficiently than to be actually producing a thing." I laugh. Very familiar; efficiency is my middle name. In various transcripts I read that intermediates get along easily with other individuals, especially in casual meetings. True for me too. Then I bump into this snippet in session 406 on relationships: "In a manner of speaking, within very physical terms, you may express to yourself, "This is requiring of too much energy," and it is not worthy of your time, and you are not inclined to be offering this much attention to another individual and their creations, for you are much more occupied with your OWN creations and your own perception. Therefore, there is an impatience with other individuals." I know enough. Intermediate I am.

One other statistic that I want to investigate before having all of them checked is the primary entry and way of information processing, which Elias calls focus type. To be clear: this is not related to a lifetime, but to information perception and processing.

There are four of them, according to Elias: emotional, thought, religious and political focus. He links them to the energy centers in their description; from session 622: "[…] emotionally focused individuals respond inwardly to information and stimulus through the yellow energy center and the responsiveness of their emotions. This is not to say that individuals that are emotionally focused do not also process information and incorporate the functions of all other types of focuses, but that they initially input and output their creations and their reality through the expression of emotion. Individuals that incorporate thought focus within a particular manifestation input and output through the action of thought initially. Those individuals that incorporate the focus of religious focus input and output through feeling; not emotion, but through feeling. Those individuals that incorporate political focus input and output through sensation."

I recognize myself mostly in the thought focus, and write that down, together with my impressions for the other statistics. Soon after I communicate my little list to a forum member who is about to have a session with Elias, who gives the following feedback on my impressions: I belong to the Sumafi family, which is not a big surprise as I am organized and focused on information gathering and sharing, and often go down to the details. I am aligned with the Sumari family, it turns out. Not so strange either, as I am not a group oriented person, I enjoy the art of writing, and I love to provoke people and to joke around. Indeed I am intermediate and my focus type is thought.

The confirmation does not imply that I have full grip on the material, as it is huge and complex. I can only say that I have some understanding of a few basic concepts. I am pleased though that my impressions have proved to be rather correct. I also appreciate having gained more insight in myself using the Elias concepts. Especially the information on the intermediate orientation I find helpful in that area; it explains my preferences as well as relationships in life rather well. Now, this is not to say that other intermediates are like me. I know one, a lovely lady who, thanks to her committed political focus and her life intent of building connections, is actively involved with other people.

I notice quite some differences between forum members with similar or even equal sets of statistics, which I find fascinating; they confirm the uniqueness of the individual. Gender appears to play a part too. For example, for a Western male it is not easy to have an emotional focus type, as social imprinting dictates a thought type in Western cultures. So he may hide that emotional functionality for many years if not lifelong, while an emotional focused female is allowed to be herself. This and other insights resulting from internalizing the basic Elias concepts widen my perception of people, which I much appreciate.

Family belonging and alignment, orientation and focus type are all present at birth, I understand. They are chosen by the focus in a pre-birth planning phase. I don't feel ready to dive into pre-birth choices and conditions yet. I first need a working knowledge of the Elias material on both consciousness basics and the creation and blueprint of the universe.

3
About origin

As a curious citizen of our physical universe, I want to know how it has come into existence, and how it is linked to consciousness. I am in for a treat. While digging into the Elias material I soon discover that there is no such thing as a beginning, as there is no such thing as time nor linearity. Consciousness is always present, and always on the move. No start, no middle, no end. Just action, in all possible ways and directions, creating physical and non-physical dimensions, forms, creatures, matter. Consciousness is everything.

To quote Elias, who for the sake of our time-focused convenience and understanding does use wordings sometimes that are time-related, but always emphasizes its absence: "[…] before the organization and orchestration of your universe, as you view it, was consciousness. Before essence, as you interpret it, was the whole. You may use any term you are wishing for this … action. I do not use the term "being" purposely, for your term of God, or All That Is, or The Creating Universal One and Whole, whatever you choose to call it, is not a being. It is all consciousness. It is an action. It incorporates all. Within this experience, of what you term to be god, are many, many elements. […] I have used, as an example, your time frame, only for your understanding; for there is no time incorporation. Also, essence did not create consciousness. Consciousness is. Consciousness creates all. I have expressed the usage of a time frame for your perception in expressing consciousness as original, and essence springing from consciousness. In actuality, there is no time frame. All is simultaneous. All is in a state of becoming, as is also the Creating Universal One and Whole, which is not completed, which is ongoing, which is present always, now." (Session 79)

In short the Creating Universal One and Whole "is a continuous action of exploration […], a type of folding in which is the exploration which creates the expansion. There is a continuous expansion. It does not concern in actuality with how it came to be, for this is a moot point, for there has been no beginning point. Therefore, it continually expresses becoming, which is the action of continuous exploration of itself. Once again, this is a distortion, for it is not an "it." It is an action." (Session 1255)

Its intent, its purpose is to be, to explore, to experience value fulfillment, Elias claims in session 144: " The intent of consciousness is to be. Within manifestations of creatures and plants, formations upon your planet, your planet itself, your universe, the intent is to be. Within this beingness, there is also held an intent for value fulfillment; for all of consciousness exists with value fulfillment. […] All of consciousness, to the extreme of each atom, each link of consciousness, exists within the intent, so to speak, of individual value fulfillment. This is to be the most fulfilled expression of its being. Therefore, its purpose is in its own beingness." Value fulfillment, in short, is what you accomplish by exploring and following your intent, I read in session 1328. And, as said above, that is not only valid for a human being, but for everything in any universe and dimension, as everything has an intent.

I conclude that the Creating Universal One and Whole, or All-That-Is in Seth's terminology, is an all-encompassing creative consciousness action, incorporating intent and value fulfillment. I decide to leave it at that. I will not use it more than strictly necessary, as the term has a connotation for us humans with a godlike being, which it clearly isn't.

¶

The consciousness elements that Elias mentions have caught my eye. I know that no separation exists, so these elements will be consciousness action too, but to understand the concept of the creation of all, I need some information on what they consist of, and how basic their function can be. In session 79 I find a description that works for me: "These elements of consciousness know no limits of time or space. You may think of these as very tiny, black holes. You may think of them, if you will, in physical terms, as elements smaller than your smallest physical particles; but these elements are that which creates all physical expression. Everything, within every universe, within every dimension, is created by these elements of consciousness; and they are everything. They are not only the driving force behind matter and action, but are matter and action also".

In later sessions, I notice, he calls these elements 'links of consciousness'. Not units, as that term implied the existence of a closed system, which consciousness is not.

I know from my old physics text books that energy is also related to action. I am wondering how energy is linked to consciousness actions. I am lucky, the term energy is being discussed on the Elias FB forum, so I don't need to look far. In session 553, Elias describes how he considers energy: "Energy is movement. Energy is motion. Therefore, energy is an action rather than a thing. […] It is the action of movement. In relation to essence, it is the movement of essence. In relation to consciousness, it is the quality of consciousness, the state of consciousness, to be continuously moving."

This information from session 333 I also find helpful: "Every expression of energy, every movement, is reality. It is a different expression and configuration of energy, of the motion, and in different combinations it is creating of different expressions of reality."

In the same session, the introduction of the element of time as a grouping of links of consciousness supports my new understanding of energy, being connected to matter as well, as Einstein pointed out in his famous formula. In Elias words: "Time is an expression of links of consciousness grouped together to be creating of a thickness which facilitates physical creations. Time is the factor that facilitates the creation of your physical dimensions: matter. Without the configuration of time, you also may not be creating of physical expressions, physical matter. But time is merely another expression of consciousness, a configuration of links of consciousness grouped together in a different organization than essence to be creating of an action that shall facilitate physical manifestations. Physical manifestations grouped together with time are the links of consciousness that are creating of certain cooperative organizations with the organizations of time, which create physical manifestations."

What or who created our physical universe, including our earth and solar system, is my next question. It turns out to be essences, which are a configuration of links of consciousness creating a personality tone. Elias defines an essence in session 191a as "the personality identification, in individuality, of consciousness", which has its own intent or direction. The function of essences is to create, and they have created this universe, I notice in the same session: "There have been essences in groups, which we identify as families, that are directly connected to the creation of this dimension and physical reality in its entirety—your entire known universe. This is only one universe, which occupies the same space arrangement as all other universes. […]"

With regards to the creation of our universe I notice a snippet from session 329 that seems worthwhile to share : "Your planet is also comprised of links of consciousness. Therefore, it IS consciousness. Therefore, it is essentially no different from yourself in that it is comprised of the same elements. The difference is that you as essence are directing of the configuration of these links of consciousness that comprise this dimension, this planet, and this particular physical universe."

Essence as director of the configuration of links of consciousness that created the dimension, this planet and our whole physical universe. I enjoy reading that; our philosophies and religions want us to look in awe at the universe, and ensure us that we are not more than tiny little specks in there, but in reality we created it.

Elias confirms our creative vastness: "Although you view yourselves to be quite limited, I continue to express to you all the tremendous diversity that is incorporated in this particular physical dimension, for you have created a blueprint in this particular physical dimension that allows for tremendous expansion and allows for tremendous freedom." (Session 1042).

The basic design of our universe, I discover while reading another transcript, is taken care of by the Dreamwalker essences, who never manifested physically themselves and don't create physical constructs. "Dreamwalkers were not, in your terms, physically manifest. Therefore, they also did not generate actual physical constructs. In a manner of speaking, the movement of the Dreamwalkers was to set a blueprint for this physical dimension, but those essences that expressed themselves in Dreamwalkers in association with this physical dimension chose not to be actually physically engaging this physical dimension. They merely designed the structure of it but not in actual physical manifestations. Their structure was the blueprint of the design of your physical dimension and, in your terms, how it would be physically manifest and produced and what the direction of it would be in its design." (Session 1203)

Dreamwalkers exist in every essence family that I comment on in the first chapter; they have a designated function which is to design blueprints, amongst others.

In summary, the purpose of our universe is to offer avenues of wide-ranging explorations, and for that a specific blueprint was designed by the Dreamwalkers. The direction into creation is taken care of by essences like you and I. More on the blueprint in the next chapter.

4
Our blueprint

Not entirely effortless I manage to get my head around the non-existence of an origin of consciousness. I dive into the blueprint session material for a solid swim. After a few hundred meters, figuratively speaking, the following question pops up in my head: where does the design come from in the first place? It basically originated in regional area 4, as this snippet in session 1557 points out:

> MARTA: "Those blueprints, they spring from where, from which area of consciousness?"
>
> ELIAS: "I would express, although this is a loose translation, it would be associated with Regional Area 4, for there are filtrations through layers of consciousness."

As I had no clue about these areas, I searched for them on the Elias web site. They were consciousness areas as this snippet from session 157 showed: "There are different areas of consciousness. These are related to attention. All of consciousness is all of consciousness. It is all the same. There are no planes. There are no levels. There are no better or higher places within consciousness. All is the same. There are different focuses of attention. In this, there are created what we term as areas of consciousness. These are not places. These are not things. They are not space. There are no sections of space that are designated as areas of consciousness. They are directions of attention. In this, they are also influenced by intent. Each essence occupies all areas of consciousness."

I giggle. So much for the myths on low and high planes in esotery, and on hell and heavens in the various religions. No ascension either, when there's no difference in consciousness. We are free as a bird, and we are enormously spread in our wideness; we are everywhere.

Back to the areas. "Regional Area one is the aspect of you in which you generate the action of physicality", Elias says in session 1357. Objective reality and awareness resides in this region.

From session 85: "Within regional area two, all physically focused consciousness, collectively and individually, is originating. All of your manifestation that is created in regional area one originates within regional area two; therefore collectively, within consciousness, your mass events also originate within this area of consciousness." So, the creation of mass events, for example wars and weather events like tornado's, stem from that region. Regional area three incorporates "transition", the residence of the focus awareness after the termination of life, as well as a so-called "collective library" where consciousness knowledge is stored.

From session 1357: "Regional Area 4 is the action of, […] in a manner of speaking, your archetype. In association with any action of generating any physical manifestation, this springs, figuratively speaking, from this whole of Regional Area 4."

Elias himself resides in area 4, he states in session 488: "I occupy my attention—of this aspect of this essence, that which you identify as this personality of Elias—within Regional Area 4, for it offers myself the opportunity to be interactive with you within Regional Area 1 without an overwhelming expression of energy translation. There be much more difficulty in expressing objective communication with all of you here within Regional Area 1 if I were to be focusing my attention within a much more far-removed Regional Area of consciousness."

There were other aspects of consciousness in the various areas that also caught my eye, like the presence or absence of a time frame. It was all very intriguing information to me.

¶

Now that I have some insight in the regional areas, I can deep dive into the blueprint material. I plunge back into the Elias web water, and discover that this blueprint consists of many features. Ours is a very complex universe.

Sexuality, emotion and duality are some of these features. Elias describes them in the following snippet from session 1179. "Now; in association with your physical dimension, the design of this physical dimension incorporates one of the base elements which is sexuality. In this physical dimension, you incorporate two base elements in the blueprint, so to speak, of your physical reality. One is sexuality; one is emotion—the in and the out, so to speak. This particular physical dimension is, in a manner of speaking, based upon duality. This is not a negative term and is not to be confused with duplicity, which is a belief system. The duality of your physical dimension incorporates two aspects or two expressions of every action, every manifestation and every expression that you incorporate within your physical reality. In association with the physical, or the outward expressions, this is defined as sexuality, which also incorporates a duality of male and female genders, which are also associated with all of your manifestations within your physical reality. Even those expressions which may not necessarily be defined as a physical manifestation are associated with gender."

He clearly states that there is a difference between duality and duplicity, the latter being a belief that we hold on people, situations, creatures, things: being good or bad, ugly or pretty, wise or dumb, and everything else stamped with judgment.

Belief systems are also part of the blueprint; they are "an intricate expression of the blueprint of this particular physical focus, this physical dimension. Without these beliefs, you may eliminate this particular dimension, for you have created this dimension with the incorporation of these beliefs for that particular type of experience. There are myriads of physical dimensions. This is merely one. This one incorporates this type of belief systems. They shall continue." (Session 819)

A belief that is directly connected to two other blueprint elements, the ones of solidity and time, is that of separation and singularity. I am aware that we always see ourselves as separated from another individual, but I am glad to find out that this perception serves a purpose: the purity of our experiences as focuses. Otherwise we wouldn't be able to focus, literally, on our lives; we would constantly be overwhelmed by the experiences and emotions of our other focuses of our essences, and by other essences and dimensions. Undoable.

The time element of our universe is accompanied by linearity. I much enjoy this snippet about their connectedness, and how linearity is related to our perception; it isn't a fixed element: "The blueprint in this reality for time is that it move in a linear fashion. But that is precisely the blueprint: that it moves in a linear fashion. In that, the blueprint does not necessarily specify how it will move in that linear fashion. Perception dictates that. Now, collectively you have agreed, to this point, that time will incorporate an even and consistent linear movement, but although to an extent that will remain, as future times are realized, there is a flexibility in that and it can be manipulated in different manners in generating it more rapidly or more slowly. And that involves perception, in which the individual experiences time more quickly or more slowly.

[…]" (Session 2536)

So, the blueprint elements for our universe, including our earth, are emotion, sexuality, duality, solidity and time. In addition, as I find out, an individual (anything) comes with a blueprint as well. Here's a snippet from session 471 on this particular blueprint that fuels my appetite to know more about the topic: "Each individual creates a type of blueprint before their engagement of manifestation in physical focus. In this, they choose a particular pool of probabilities which creates a particular desire of direction of movement." Pre-birth planning! My personality much enjoys to plan and organize. I will certainly dive into this activity; details will follow.

I have touched upon very basic creation information in this chapter and the previous one. The most important concept to me is the one related to the links of consciousness that are involved in the creation of everything, everywhere. I notice that I need a break from the pure theoretical concepts and the high information density, and decide to embark the ship of my consciousness adventures, with an intent to link them to the Elias material.

5
Consciousness adventures

Using the Elias material for this book, and for the purpose of widening my own awareness, is not a coincidence. My openness to extracurricular information sources has quite a history which started at a young age with my dream recall. My dreams were and continue to be a source of laughter and surprise in my family because of their liveliness. I enjoy them as well, as long as they are not nightmarish. They play out in a movie style which makes it relatively easy to remember and to relate to them. Often my dreams have this mundane, close to life quality which I do not consider very interesting. So I didn't write them down until about eight years ago, when I felt triggered to start a dream diary. A probable cause for the trigger was my participation in my first program at the Monroe Institute a few months earlier, where I became familiar with conscious out-of-body traveling, a kind of dreaming awake. The hemi-sync technology that TMI uses to relax the mind and open it to wider awareness has worked excellent for me. I must add here that by then I was already open and used to working with alternative information sources thanks to mediumistic and psychic sessions that I had held for a few years.

In that first program, called Gateway, I went on all kinds of out-of-body adventures in consciousness realms I had not visited before, at least not consciously. There was one adventure that opened my eyes for good to the possibility that in life many and even opposite features and qualities exist side by side in one person, animal, event, and what have you. I usually perceived just one side of a coin. Roles in life are not fixed and polarity only exists in our heads, was my conclusion back then. It was a funny awareness widening adventure of which I was an observer only, and I want to share it with you here:

> *A movie pops up of three bunnies, molesting a fox on a field of grass; they even kick him all over the lawn, and laugh viciously. Then they are sitting on the fox, pulling his ears and having a blast; the fox looks very sad. Suddenly the bunnies stop the bullying. They put their arms around the fox, and the four of them walk towards the forest, laughing together and having fun.*

I shared this account with the other group members in the exercise evaluation round. They laughed a lot, and much valued the wisdom in the adventure.

In my other out-of-body trips I was often accompanied by an eagle that showed itself in front of my mental eyes while I was usually still in the process of deepening the trance state. It clearly couldn't wait to go flying with me. Its presence in those trips gave me a sense of being accompanied and guided in my awareness adventures, which I much appreciated. A wonderful program for me for that matter as well. I was very glad I had attended it.

The reason for my participation was that I wanted to experience out of body traveling following Robert Monroe's footsteps, in preparation for my book on free will after life. My ultimate goal was to experience the afterlife realms. To be able to achieve that I noticed I had to participate in a few other programs of the Monroe Institute as well, which I did. In my second program, Guidelines, I was able to increase my trust in myself.

I used to separate myself in compartments in those days, with a higher spiritual self on some hierarchical top, which is reflected in the trip account below. No hierarchy exists in life, though, as I have stated in previous chapters.

> *I meet my higher self and the eagle, on which/whom I fly to a very pleasant place. I think that the first energy form I meet is my grandma, or a person strongly connected to her. We meet for just a very short while, after which the eagle takes me to a nice place in the sun. The atmosphere is loving and everything is well. I feel fine. A man appears, who I don't know, but my higher self does. He is serious and makes a worried impression. They talk about something, but I can't hear it. I'm still in a happy mood and totally trust that my higher self is taking care of everything. It feels like I am being taken care of, and that I don't have to do anything, just as a child.*

I felt very satisfied with my trust in being taken care of by myself, and with the possible meet-up with my deceased grandma. I had clearly touched the afterlife realm in my trip. In a subsequent program, Lifeline, dedicated to the afterlife realms I had several encounters with deceased people in their various emotional and mental states during my out-of-body travels. One of those involved a meeting with a male spirit with interesting info and the creation of my own place in an afterlife realm:

> *Then I met Joe [a fellow student in the program] on a bench and sat down next to him. A male spirit arrived, telling me that there's not much difference between earthly and non-earthly mental activity. So below, so above. The differences are per individual, not per dimension.*

Within focus 27 I went to create a special place. First I created a lovely garden with several levels. There was grass, plants, bushes and higher up also trees. On the lowest level I created a swimming pool. On the top level I put my house with a lot of light and separate bedrooms for my visitors. Behind the house there's wood. Somewhere in the middle of the garden there's a bench, in the grass, with a view of the swimming pool and of the juicy grass fields outside my garden where all kinds of animals are walking around and passing by, including elephants, lions and tigers. Also there are people who take care of these animals.

Then Bob's voice is back into the headphones, asking me to put a big recognition sign in my special place. I place a big shield in the garden, with "J's Paradise" on it, printed on both sides, only visible when necessary, for me and others.

I much enjoyed the experience.

The creation of the dream diary turned out to be useful, as it improved the recall of details and allowed me to recognize themes when re-reading them. After participating in those three programs the dreams became more interesting to me. For example, in a period of six weeks in early 2010 I had four dreams that had clear precognitive characteristics. One involved a course that I had signed up for in 3D reality. I was attending it in a dream and it didn't go well, which turned out to be true 6 months later. Another dream indicated the non-commitment of my landlord in a renovation project; that situation played out in reality too. In a third dream I smelled smoke from the apartment below me, and I went downstairs to check the situation; he had closed down the fire by then. That literally happened one year later in real life. And last but least a loved one was laid off by his actual employer in a dream, and two years later he was indeed fired.

My memory within dreams seemed to improve as well. In this dream I recognize the scenery from a previous dream:

> *I was [again] at the course I was going to attend a month later, and everything there was different from usual. The institute had different buildings, and I had a different task, that of presenting the course. I didn't perform well at that task, the female instructor told me. She was right in that: I forgot to say several things, and was too late a few times. At some point we had a meeting in a house a few kilometers from the main building, as that house had an extra floor in it. I walked towards that place with a few others, ahead of the rest of the group. We arrived in an urban area at some booths where illegal copies of software were sold, amongst other goods in which a course participant was interested. We were a bit lost on our way, but the surroundings rather resembled those in a dream I had had about a month earlier, so I was aware there was a school in the neighborhood. Just a while later I saw that school, and knew where we were.*

Most of my dreams in my past and present are related to current emotional and mental states. My friends and family members often participate. In addition I have dreams in which individuals take part that I don't know at all in daily life. My dream friends or maybe friends in other focuses. Also tv characters feature in some dreams. Especially Leroy Jethro Gibbs, senior investigator and team lead of NCIS, has presented himself regularly; NCIS is a CBS broadcasted tv series on the law enforcement organization called Naval Criminal Investigation Services. Initially he had a guidance or authority role in my dreams, but in recent times he has featured in any kind of role. When I noticed that change, I first felt a bit abandoned, then I realized that I might no longer feel much need for an outside directive force. That realization took place while reading the Seth book on dreams and projections of consciousness about two years ago.

The awareness of my own power catapulted me into performing some dream exercises from that book, which led to the following dream about the endless possibilities we have in life, symbolized by different styles in make-up, hair and clothing:

> *A make-up show is taking place at a location that I don't know, with people I don't know either. It evolves around the color dark blue. That color hardly fits any woman's face, it appears, except maybe for those with dark brown hair. A solution is presented: a mix of that dark blue with other colors. The girl who undergoes the experiment with the dark blue also receives a drawing of a pair of small glasses on one side of her face; drawings can be added to face make up too, is the message of the artist. The girl laughs about it, but doesn't really like the result. Suddenly she is wearing dungarees, in a flash moment. Also it appears to be possible to add different blond colors in hair, also at the same time, even for one day.*

The dream reminded me of the mental movie with the bunnies and the fox that I described in the section above. I liked the message of broad possibilities. However, I was less happy with my recurring dreams of being in a potentially or outright dangerous situation. I had had them for several years now. They often took place in my bedroom or on the roof next to it, where I supposedly couldn't escape from. Luckily I always woke up before the situation got out of hand, and I would find myself in bed or next to it, reaching for the light-switch with a racing heart. These nightmares usually took place in the early hours of the night. It took me ages to link them to my digestive issues, as I mostly didn't write down the situation around a dream, and when I did I forgot about it. They were just too confronting and frequent. Inspired by the Seth exercises I added the circumstances from daily life to my dream diary. It did not take me too long to discover the link between the no-escape nightmares and the state of my physical body digesting some unwanted substance, often fatty or spicy food. Also I noticed a simultaneous link between those dreams and stress from tough and insecure times, for example in relationships with people. The combination of the difficulty to digest both unsuited food and emotional stress was the main trigger for the creation of the nightmares, was my conclusion. The awareness of this 'lethal' combination helped a lot, judging from the drop in the frequency of the nightmares. Since then, when I have had one I always do a quick check: what did I eat, and what made me feel unsafe the day before or a few days earlier.

There may well be other factors involved in the creation of the nightmares, but I do not feel an urge to investigate into them. Instead I prefer to research what Elias has to say on dreams and out-of-body experiences.

6
Out-of-body

So, what is Elias' take on dreams and out-of-body experiences in general? They are obviously similar in the core, judging from this snippet from session 151: "You accomplish out-of-body states many, many times. Your objective in this is to be objectively consciously aware, and remembering and understanding of this action. It is not a question of how to do this or whether you do this, for you do this continuously. Each time you experience yourself drifting, you are experiencing your out-of-body [state]. Every time you engage your sleep state, without exception, you engage out-of-body experience. This is your communication with essence."

Essentially we are out-of-body a lot. The main difference between a dream and a deliberate out-of-body trip or projection may well be the amount of objective awareness involved. I decide to limit my focus to dream research, and bump into a lot of material. In fact, too much and too deep to get an immediate grip on it. While wondering where to begin, I notice this little snippet from session 92: "All consciousness engages this state; not only what you view to be alive, within your terms; not only your animals, yourselves, your plants; your plants do dream; but all atoms, molecules, particles [...] and all engage within a dream state, for all employ both elements of subjective and objective selves." So everything on earth dreams. That is an eye-opener for me.

The subjective and objective self that are mentioned in the snippet catches my attention. Elias explains them as follows in the same session: "All altered states of consciousness, such as your dream state, your state within out-of-body experiences, and all other altered [states of] consciousness, as you view them, including your view of "subconscious", shall be referred to as subjective consciousness or self. Subjective self is the creative aspect, the initiating aspect, of your manifestation. Objective self is the experiencing and executing element of your manifestation." Also, from that same session: "As there is no time element within the subjective self, you may view the interaction, from the standpoint of the objective self, as reversed. You may dream, and to your perception it is seeming that you have been dreaming of what has been occurring within your previous day. There is no time element within your subjective self. It is an interpretation of the objective self."

That means that it is possible to have so called precognitive dreams as well, in the perspective of the objective self or awareness. For the subjective self everything in life takes place simultaneously though. That makes me think about the dreams that I have termed precognitive earlier on. To my objective self they are indeed indicating of future events, but in the grand scheme of consciousness they are taking place in the moment. In one occasion, a few years back, the dream and the objective event are placed very close to each other:

> *I was hanging out with a dream friend in a city environment. We were sitting by a pool that belonged to a hotel building and suddenly a shark came out of the depth of the pool and tried to attack us. We were just fast enough to pull away from the pool, so it couldn't harm us. It laughed viciously and told us that it might not have succeeded to kill us, but it had surely done something that would make us feel miserable. The female friend and I were shocked at*

its appearance and viciousness. We left the pool area and the dream ended.

Lo and behold, in the morning of the next day I got stomach and intestinal issues. Only then I recognized the link with the dream, and I remembered that I had eaten fish the evening before. This was such a clear chain of events, the rotten fish for dinner, then the rotten (in character) shark in the dream followed by the light food poisoning, that I had to laugh wholeheartedly despite feeling rather unwell.

What is a dream, actually? In Elias' words in session 1771: "Now; dreams are the objective awareness participation in subjective activity. It is an action in which you are translating the subjective activity into imagery, and that creates dreams. The significant element to create dream imagery is to involve the objective awareness." I had been creating very vividly. The shark, the pool, my friend and I sitting there, and the events taking place in the dream, that would be the dream imagery that made up the dream.

This snippet from session 324 clarifies this translation activity and adds a communication aspect to it: "Your dream state is a translation of imagery in itself. It is a communication period between yourself as a focus of essence and the whole of essence, and within this communication, as it does not appear in language but is transmitted through energy impulses, you translate this into imagery that you are familiar with within your physical focus. Therefore, within your dream state you hold images of individuals, of houses, of water, of actions, of creatures. You do not image objects that are entirely unfamiliar to you, for where shall you draw upon—within what you think of as your imagination—these pictures? Your attention is focused here. Therefore, your translation is focused here, into elements that you may understand."

The translation activity also takes place in lucid dreams: "Lucid dreaming is merely an action of allowing oneself to be engaging the objective awareness in the action of the subjective awareness. But it continues to be a translation and not necessarily objectively accurate, for it is imagery; therefore it is abstract. In subject matter it may be accurate, but in details it is abstract and requires interpretation." (session 1171)

So I create my dreams in the dream state, by translating subjective activity into elements and events that I can recognize objectively. That is not too difficult to grasp. I don't know very well what to think about the dream state though, apart from that it apparently is an altered state of consciousness. I dive into the material again and find this piece of information from session 111, that adds people and a regional area dimension to the story: "[The dream state] is the expression of your subjective self speaking to you, which engages all of your probable selves and focuses. It also directly connects to information within Regional Area Two. It also holds the ability to connect with other individuals or essences, as you may term this, within transition, or [a] wider [awareness] of yourself. You tap tremendous information within your dream state."

My dreams are usually packed with people, and now it seems possible that some of those that I don't know in daily life may well be other focuses or probable selves; whatever these selves are I will look into later, I decide. My objective self is so focused on this physical universe dimension that I would never have thought of that myself.

I am meeting other essences in my dreams also, as I am well aware of. Some of them I know, they are my friends and family, but maybe there are also people that I will never meet face to face in daily life. How exciting to have such extended social life at night!

To my delight I discover even more connections in session 74: "Be remembering also, that there is continuous interaction between your dream state and your waking state, and not only for you individually; for your dream state, at other levels, so to speak, incorporates other individuals also; and although you may not view yourselves to be interacting personally, with certain other individuals or groups of individuals within consciousness, you are, continually. Therefore, this is reflected within your dream state."

¶

This snippet in session 28 clearly connects the dream state with regional area two: "Your dream state is contained within regional area two. Your impulses, your creativity, your connections, are expressed and manifest from this area to physical focus." That is good to know. Clearly it isn't just mass events that are stemming from this area.

In session 32, an example of the link between the waking state and a dream is provided: "[…] your interaction back and forth between regional areas one and two is constant. It is going on continuously, every day. Within regional area one, you experienced a remembering of a song from a dream. Within regional area two, circumstances were all engineered and fit together to allow this same song to be playing on your radio at your job, while you were working, to allow you to connect. All things are created initially within regional area two. All of your circumstances, all of your coincidences, all of your choices originate in this area of consciousness, which is connected to all other physically focused individuals."

Now we are talking! The continuous interconnectedness between the waking state in area one and the dream state in area two is a basic feature of life. I have read before, in books on shamanic concepts, that dreams are considered fundamental by shamans with regards to creations in life, and now I have found information of how the links are engineered in area two.

I feel very excited about the insights that I have gained on dreams and out-of-body experiences, and am ready to reach for a larger picture of essence.

7
Essence essentials

Essence is crucial for us, humans, as the information in previous chapters shows. It is a configuration of links of consciousness, it creates non-stop and stands at the base of our physical universe, amongst others, as this snippet from session 2550 states: "There is not actually a difference between the identification of essence and consciousness. They are not two separate things or entities. Essence is an expression of consciousness that is the manipulating aspect of consciousness that creates in association with physical manifestations."

We consist of essence, we are essence. Individual personalities with an immense bandwidth. This general picture is thrilling to me, and it generates a desire within me to know a few details too. For example on how an essence is created. Apparently this creation is the outcome of a fragmentation action, as Elias states in session 486: "Now; at times, two or more essences may merge together, and within that mergence, there may be created a combined quality of those essences that chooses, through its desire, to be its own individual essence, and within agreement, there is what is created to be a fragmentation process, so to speak. [...] The action of fragmentation is instantaneous. [...] In this, as several essences merge together and are overlapping within consciousness, the combination of those essences—which is occurring in this situation—creates new qualities, for it is a combining of different qualities within different essences; different attributes which are expressed, not necessarily latent."

In the same session Elias mentions an important reason for such action: "Now; in this action, certain qualities of those essences may hold a desire to be expressing themselves and exploring avenues of consciousness within their own direction and design, and therefore, there is a desire to be fragmented and to be creating of a new essence which shall choose its independent, in a manner of speaking, direction of movement."

When the fragmentation is finished, which should not be taken as the end of a process as the action is instantaneous as mentioned above, the essence will commence its exploration. One way to do so is to create focuses, which is Elias' term for a life personality, in case the essence is interested in manifesting in a physical universe. Not all essences want that, but the ones that created us have chosen this physical route, usually alongside non-physical routes. Many essences have focuses in several dimensions, physical and non-physical, I learn while reading quite a few session transcripts. This snippet from session 459 illustrates the multiplicity of their attention: "Essences are very diverse in their attention. Some essences choose not to be experiencing physical dimensions at all. Some essences choose to be engaging the exploration of physical dimensions. Therefore, those essences which are choosing to be interactive in physical dimensions would hold more of a knowing of each other in these areas of attention than would those that are not choosing to engage that type of experience."

Many essences know each other, and they radiate towards each other in tone and interests, just like we do, as focuses on earth. Like seeks like on that wide level of consciousness too, as this snippet from the same session suggests: "In reality, there is a knowing of all essences, but there is also, figuratively speaking, more of a knowing or recognition of some essences than other essences, and this would be a byproduct of similar tones, and also the manifestation of many similar directions in attention."

Not only do they know each other, they are in constant interaction with each other too, which, as said, sometimes results in a fragmentation action. The interactions take place in the non-physical, but may be noticed in a physical world like ours as well if these essences have focuses here, as session 836 suggests: "As an example, an essence may choose another essence to be merging with, and accessing certain qualities of the other essence that shall be challenging to the first essence. Now; this may translate in physical manifestations and expressions as manifesting several or many focuses of attention with each other that may express an interaction of conflict, or it may be expressed in a type of challenging that shall be expressed in agitation. But this is a physical translation of the interaction which is occurring between these two essences in non-physical expressions, which may not be expressed quite in the same manner as the translation appears within physical focuses."

Luckily, also more pleasant interactions bleed through physically; from the same session: "Now; in another example, an essence may choose to be interactive with another essence, accessing qualities of them both to be expressing what YOU in physical terms identify as a tenderness. This may be a merging of energies to be creating certain types of experiences and sharing certain energy expressions, and the translation in physical terms may be the creation of several or many focuses of attention together that express affection or gentleness, or as you term it, tenderness in physical manifestations."

I continue my investigations and discover that when an essence directs energy into the physical world, this is called a physical manifestation and the result is a focus, an incarnation, a human life. The essence that performs this action is called the directing essence. In addition a phenomenon called the observing essence exists. This is an essence that accompanies the focus during its entire lifetime, or during a part of it. Apparently it is as involved with the focus as the directing essence, this snippet of session 1772 shows: "The observing essence experiences the focus in the same manner as the directing focus. They are generating the same experience. [...] The observing essence is merged with that focus, and therefore is that individual and is experiencing in the same manner as the directing essence. It is the choice of the focus which essence it incorporates as itself. The focus can choose to change which is the directing essence."

An observing essence is literally that: "Now; in this, you may allow yourself the recognition of the assimilation of experience through the participation of observance, for your essence allows itself the fullness of the experience in its entirety within that time framework, so to speak, without directing the focus." (Session 772) It chooses to observe instead of manifesting fully in a focus of itself, but it is still very closely linked to the focus that it is observing. Potentially interesting, but I feel that I lack the motivation to dive deeper into this topic at this moment and decide to give it a long rest. What I do find very important was that last bit about the focus to be in the choosing position, and not essence. Elias confirms this position in an outspoken manner in session 1599: "You are not OWNED by an essence; you are not CONTROLLED by essence; you ARE essence. Therefore, YOU choose."

So I am a focus and at the same time I am essence, and I am directing of the choices in my life. This is all very nice and interesting, but who am I, as an essence?

That question has become more interesting since our mind trip group was formed. We, five members of the Elias forum, started the group a year ago out of an interest in our shared focuses, the lifetimes in which we also were in contact as a group. Every week we make a trip, usually on Thursday.

At our get-togethers we use an online chat box to communicate with each other. We meet in that chat box, then set a destination, go into a meditational trance and travel for about 15 minutes with the intent to collect impressions of that destination. After that time period we meet up again in the chat box and share our impressions. We especially look for synchs in time and place and action. The results are astonishing and give us a feeling that we are connected on a much wider scale than just in this lifetime, through our essences.

At the same time a new wave of channeling, or energy exchange, is emerging. Not only Elias, but also an essence by the name of Tompkin is now actively communicating, through a lady called Tara Shaw who lives in Australia. We learn that Tompkin is closely connected with Elias. They are both part of a group of twelve essences with a shared intent, which is to help our physical universe through the shift by lessening its trauma. Each of these twelve essences contribute in their own way. Elias, for example, does this through the sharing of information with the least distortion.

For the sake of having a complete name picture of the twelve essences, I look them up on the Elias website. They are: Rose, Ordin, Twylah, Ayla, Tompkin, Otha, Elias, Patel, Lazour, Seth (channeled by Jane Roberts), Ruburt (Jane's essence), Joseph (Jane's husband Robert Butts' essence).

While searching through the material about the shift, it becomes clear that it is a change, a shift in consciousness, which will lead to a new reality for the individuals in this universe, a reality in which the individual will be aware of its essence and its interconnectedness with consciousness and all other individuals. The sense of separation will disappear. We will have enhanced capabilities in directing our consciousness that will allow us to visit other dimensions as well as the inhabitants of those dimensions, for example loved ones that have died. From session 270: "You wish to engage an individual that has disengaged physical focus. You shall hold the ability to be in active communication and interaction with another focus .. in non-physical communication. Your abilities for mobility through consciousness shall exceed any known element that you hold presently."

Our group is interested a lot in creating such encounters, and we love those weekly sessions. Not only are we active in broadening our understanding and knowledge of other focuses of ourselves in those meditation, we also set intents to meet them in our dreams.

I am intrigued at the thought of talking to a ghost, as our group lovingly calls them, so I arrange a phone appointment with Tara, and get all excited about it. When I call her the following week we chat for a while and then she goes into a deep trance state in which she is no longer aware of her surroundings. Tompkin comes through easily and clearly, and it is a pleasure to talk to him. We both have a lively and enthusiastic kind of personality which creates an instant bond.

In the session I am informed by Tompkin that I am a quick moving essence in my contacts with other people:

> TOMPKIN: "[...] you are more internally focused at the moment. And you are very quick at gaining the assistance and the information that you needed from the person you engaged. You efficiently gather that information, you say your thank you's on every level and then you move on. And it is not that you do not enjoy people. It is simply that you are a bit, excuse the terminology, hell-bent in your direction and you are so focused in that movement that it is a bit like a bull ploughing through a field of cows. [...] As that is how your energy moves.

And you are merely holding brief conversations with each cow as you quickly pass through them all, if you know what I am saying. How is that for imagery?" (Laughing)

JANTINE: (Laughing) "Thank you for this picture. I can relate to that. Is that something that belongs to my essence or is that something that I chose to do as a focus?

TOMPKIN: "Both. Your essence travels much in this way. You are very, very quick, light speed really. Most people have difficulty in keeping up." (Private session)

Due to social constructs with regards to the importance of long relationships, I have mixed feelings about my short relationships with people, but I accept my contact style after a short while. It is part of who I am, at all levels: goal-oriented. As Tompkin confirms in that same session: "Yes, this is how your essence operates. Once it is on a quest there is no interruption."

I also want to know from which essence my own essence is fragmented. This is his answer: "One moment. You are fragmented from Twylah. […] And this is why you often have excesses of energy, exuberance and your joyful nature, for Twylah is very much the same. […] With Twylah she does prefer the more positive female energy and also, you choose a similar resonance to her. […] You as Adell." Twylah is one of those twelve essences as well, as mentioned in a section above. Adell is my essence name.

From Lawrence whom I contact a few months later via Nuno I receive some extra link-related information: apparently a very common trait in my focus personalities, which my essence projects into the focuses, is that of playfulness, which I derive from Twylah as well.

He also tells me that my essence theme is creativity. The theme does not run through all of my focuses, he adds; "it it is more of an aspect which the essence is accentuating." (Private session)

By the way, Lawrence is a discarnate essence who is fragmented from Patel and channeled by Nuno Romao, a fellow Elias forum member.

¶

Next on the menu are my other focuses. I have written down my impressions about the ones I have observed in dreams and mind travels, and am eager to check them. It is not a goal of mine to get a complete picture of all of my focuses. I just want to get a feel of a couple of them, and to see how they are linked to the other members in the our group.

Checks with Tompkin, Elias and Lawrence confirm that my focus impressions are mostly accurate.

My list includes amongst others two camel herder focuses, one in Morocco and one in Afghanistan, sixteen (!) archeologists, one focus in Australia, a future focus not residing on earth, and a future and a past focus in China. In addition I have several focuses in the USA, usually alive in the last century; one of them is a navy crime investigator in the same role as special agent Gibbs in NCIS. I enjoy hearing that from Tompkin, who also tells me that I occupy a very similar function in another focus, in Japan; both focuses have disengaged by now, he adds. Furthermore I have a WW II focus in Amsterdam, an art historian in Paris, a focus in the Amazonian jungle, and a few focuses in Turkey, 2000 years ago. And many more, of course.

I become rather interested in the geographical spread

of my focuses. Tompkin had informed me that 498 of them were based in the USA, which explains my love for visiting this large country rather well. It often feels like home when I am there. I ask the essence Lawrence about my other locations. From our first session:

> JANTINE: "[...] I am very much wondering what the locations of my other focuses in general are. I am aware that about 500 of them are in the USA. So I was wondering where are the other focuses located? Is that more or less throughout the globe or do I have most focuses in Europe or in Africa or Latin America?"
>
> LAWRENCE: "I would express that the majority of your focuses in present time frames and in recent time frames and to some extent in future time frames as you view it, many of your focuses are either in the US or that geographic region, as well as in Western Europe. Some in Asia. Those would be the primary locations."
>
> *(Private session)*

So, I am basically a Western-society-oriented essence. Good to know. My concurrent focuses, alive in the same time framework as I am, may be looking quite similar, Elias says in session 345: "Many times, essences, in focusing several focuses within one time framework, shall be manifesting in very similar manners. Therefore, many times the appearance physically of the individuals shall be quite similar, but as with all other creations, this is not a rule. Therefore, some essences may be creating several focuses within one time framework, and they may bear no resemblance physically to each other. Generally, they shall be creating similarities in appearance with all of their different focuses within one time framework, but as I have stated, this is not a rule."

Interestingly enough, this physical similarity is exactly the reason why Tracy, one of the focus exploration group members, while researching the city of Amsterdam on the internet, recognizes my female WW II focus on a photograph. Tompkin confirms this focus in a follow-up session, and I congratulate and thank my exploration friend for this excellent find. I research this focus via Google, and it turns out that she and I have lived in Amsterdam rather side by side for about 15 years. She is diseased now, but I would have loved to meet her!

With Tracy and the other ones from the group we turn out to have many focuses together, group focuses as we call them. Several in Turkey, various in the USA and Europe, one in Afghanistan, one in China, one in the Amazon, the future one I mention above, and various others. We love to find out about them, and most of our shared focus impressions are confirmed by one of the ghosts, as we call the channeling essences lovingly. Our essences are very close, obviously.

In total we have 726 focuses together, Elias has told us. This doesn't mean that in all of them the five of us are present; two focuses together also constitute a group focus. We share focuses in all kind of capacities, such as family members, friends, and I am assuming we are enemies as well in some of them.

I share focuses with my family and friends as well, it turns out. And not just one, they are many. I am pleased with this discovery. It makes me feel deeply connected to them, which apparently is one of the goals of the shift: the awareness of connectedness. A bonus.

In a session with Elias we discuss the topic of focus counts as well, in our three-dimensional universe as well as in other dimensions:

ELIAS: "I would express that it would be exceedingly difficult to express a count of focuses that are not in this physical dimension, but I would express that you are increasing your number of focuses in this dimension."

JANTINE: "Right. And what number are they up to currently?"

ELIAS: "Remember that focuses in this dimension are not limited to your world."

JANTINE: "I know this."

ELIAS: "I would express that you have expanded this to approximately almost 2000."

(Private session)

Expanding! I am obviously enjoying the exploration of this universe.

All this talk about shared focuses and focus counts makes me eager to gain knowledge on how a focus comes to life. This is the topic of the next chapter.

8
The creation of a focus

How and why do we, human beings, come into existence? These questions have fascinated me long before I started investigating into the Elias material. Also Eastern and Western philosophies and religions seem to enjoy researching the origin of a human life, but I am not impressed by their answers; I consider them too determinist. My zest for choice has brought me to Jane's Seth books and more recently to the Elias material, and I am determined to find out what Elias mentions on those pre-life topics.

I dive into the material to get an idea on what is involved in the preparation of a life. What catches my eye immediately is Elias' emphasis on the upcoming focus being a new creation, not a re-incarnation of a former focus: "You are a new creation. You, physically manifest, are individual and new and perfect, and shall never be repeated, as you are not repeating another. You are your own individual personality manifest physically, which shall continue and which has always continued previously." (Session 131)

No linearity or sequence; focuses can be inserted in any time frame: "Re-manifestation is not reincarnation. They are entirely different elements, for there is no reincarnation. You also think in terms of sequence, which this also holds no relevance within non-physical terms." (Session 136).

I notice that there are different avenues that lead to the creation of a focus. One of these avenues, which is mentioned most often in the transcripts, starts in the afterlife phase of another focus of the same essence, like in session 147: "As you move through consciousness and you move into the area of transition, many events occur. You also continue, as always, to be making choices. Within these choices you may choose to be re-manifesting, although you do not re-manifest, for each focus is a new creation! [...] You may choose to be re-manifesting and you may accomplish this in many different directions. You may choose to be remanifesting an aspect of yourself, as you identify yourself. Or, you may be choosing to be interacting with another focus or another essence and you may together re-manifest a combination of aspects, which shall be you but shall not be you, for it shall be its own new creation. You may fragment and you may allow this fragment to re-manifest, which is you but is not you; for all aspects, all fragments, all focuses contain all of essence."

So many choices, even after life! Apparently there are some limitations too: in case the disengaged focus is holding on to strong beliefs, these beliefs may be transferred to the newly created focus: "This individual has held many very strong belief systems within this particular focus. This individual also chooses re-manifestation. Therefore, there are aspects of the belief systems that shall be, in the most probable probability, retained and held into the new manifestation, although be understanding that each focus is a new creation." (Session 272)

The other avenue is the creation of a focus by two essences: "I may express to that quite simply, you may view that two different essences may choose to be experiencing a particular pool of probabilities, and each of these essences choose to be projecting their attention into a physical manifestation within this dimension. Their intent in that particular individual focus may be the same, but their approach or angle of that intent may be expressed slightly differently, for those two particular essences may be belonging to two different families. Therefore, there is an agreement that energy shall be projected, and in mergence, the two essences shall create a focus of attention together. In this, it shall create one manifestation, one focus. That focus may at times fluctuate in its attention of its expression of its individual intent as influenced by different families and alignments. It may also hold its attention at times more in alignment with one tone, and more in alignment within other time frameworks of another tone, for it incorporates both." (Session 567)

¶

I am intrigued to find out more and make an appointment with Nuno to talk to Lawrence. In the session I ask Lawrence about how a focus is created, and this is his answer: "Let us begin with what a focus is. A focus is a projection of essence; it is a very specific projection in that all aspects of essence are far too expansive to be contained within one focus. Therefore each focus is a very specific aspect of essence in many ways. For example it accentuates certain personality traits. It has specific intents in the focus, which are an aspect of essence, however concentrated in this one focus. Now what occurs is that again essence projects simultaneously into the dimension several or many focuses simultaneously and each one of these incorporates a different aspect of essence to different degrees and different manners in great variety for again the purpose of projecting into a dimension is to acquire that experience, and to maximize this experience a great variety of focuses are projected with different characteristics." (Private session)

I notice I have not asked Lawrence when essence creates a focus, so I ask Elias. It turns out to be related to interest in participating in a specific reality:

> JANTINE: "[...] when does an essence decide upon creating a new focus? Does a disengaged focus

influence this decision?"

ELIAS: "No, I would express that if an essence is adding focuses, or subtracting, it is a matter of interest in that reality and it is not influenced of any particular focus and it is not influenced by the experiences of a particular focuses. It is a choice of you as essence in relation to your interest in that reality. If your interest increases at some point it is likely that you would add focuses. If your interest diminishes then it is likely that you would decrease focuses."

(Private session)

Interestingly enough, this information seemingly does not concur with what is said in session 147 in the section above, about a deceased focus making the decision to create a new focus, or a set of new focuses. However, if I take into account that all focuses are essence, also after a physical manifestation, it is probably just a matter of "to-may-to to-mah-to."

The new knowledge on how and when focus creation takes place in general, leads me to the next questions: what is the purpose of a focus in its physical manifestation? And what is involved in its preparation phase?

The overall purpose for any focus is experience, exploration. In addition, Elias says "within each individual focus you also hold individual intents, and as you hold these intents you create desires, and within this you create probabilities to choose from within a pool aligning with your intent. [...] You have chosen an intent which creates a direction; and in this you follow, through your experiences, this intent. The intent is what is directing of your experiences." (Session 153)

The intent appears to be a basic guideline for the upcoming manifestation, judging from that snippet. It actually consists of two intents, as stated in session 383: "Let me express to you that within each particular focus, you hold two intents which move in harmony to each other. You hold the intent of the family that you are belonging to, and you hold an individual intent which is quite influenced by the family that you are aligned with. The alignment intent is that intent which shall be more overtly expressed within your focus. The underlying intent—or the detailed aspects of your intent—shall be the expressions of the family of which you belong." As a side note, an individual might choose to align with the same consciousness family as it belongs to, for any reason.

Sometimes experience as such is chosen as the intent for the physical manifestation, with no additional goals: "You do choose some focuses without a specific aligned intent other than experience. These will be your experienced focuses that you may think of within your thought processes as your "drifting through" focuses; blissfully ignorant, in your terms, of anything other than the experiences themselves." (Session 153)

Well, not in my case. My intent is larger than just experiencing life: to be in a balanced set of both physical and mental movement and relaxation, as confirmed by Tompkin and Lawrence. I want to know how my Sumafi belonging and Sumari alignment fit into that intent, and wonder if I maybe have an additional intent in that respect. Lawrence tells me it is all included in my one single intent:

> JANTINE: "[...] I also have an intent exploring metaphysics, as I am a Sumafi, and I like to investigate, and I am Sumari aligned. I also think that as a Sumari-aligned I write down the results of the investigations for that part of the intent. Is that correct?"

LAWRENCE: "Yes, and it is an aspect of the intent as you have expressed, for in your movement of relaxation as an ease, the manner which one moves that matter, particularly so in ease, involves a knowledge, or a knowing, of what you term metaphysics, a knowing of how you operate, how you create you experience."

JANTINE: "Right. And that would be the Sumafi part?"

LAWRENCE: "I would say it is neither Sumafi or a particular aspect of your family alignment . It is simply an aspect of your intent."

(Private session)

Now that we are discussing alignment anyway, I want to know why I have chosen the Sumari family for that. Lawrence tells me it "is chosen shall we say to be different from another focus and it may be that certain aspects of this alignment then assist your intent." He apparently does not regard the belonging and alignment family as strongly contributing to the intent, at least not to my intent.

Pre-life choices with regards to the orientation, focus type, core truth(s), and more, are not necessarily related to the accomplishment of the intent, but rather to establish the personality of the focus, as Lawrence points out in this snippet:

JANTINE: "[...] My intent, did that kind of dictate my choice of orientation, my focus type, my core truth, etcetera?"

LAWRENCE: "Those are all aspects of the focus as it was projected, which I spoke of, and these characteristics then were the ones chosen for your particular focus."

JANTINE: "They were chosen to fulfill the intent?"

LAWRENCE: "To varying degrees. Other focuses of yours may have similar intents but with different characteristics. And again that would have an effect upon the manner in which the focus follows that intent. [...] you may refer to [these characteristics] as personality."

(Private session)

Core truths are very strong beliefs that the individual takes for granted as truths. They are closely linked to personal preferences. The core truth(s) that are chosen pre-life often turn into guidelines for the individual's behavior, into the basis for their preferences and opinions during life. A core truth can be justice, harmony, judgment, image, and so forth. My core truths are balance and truthfulness, Lawrence tells me. They are easy to relate to. Everything in life, and especially in my life, needs to be balanced in my opinion. With regards to the truthfulness truth: I strongly prefer to avoid lying and being lied to, but I accept and express a little white lie when I feel it's for a good cause.

¶

While scrolling through the transcripts about pre-life choices, I discover that there are more considerations involved in the preparation phase than the ones I have mentioned above. The focus also has to choose its parents and siblings, as well as the location of early life. The choice of parents is considered important by Elias, due to the enormous influence that parents have in the individual's life: "As you enter into any physical manifestation, you acquaint yourself with the physical manifestation of your parents. You choose these individuals quite carefully, in alignment with your individual intent and the direction that you are choosing to follow within probabilities within your individual focus; for these individuals that you shall manifest born to shall be quite instrumental with you, and shall be influencing quite heavily within your experience." (Session 173) In the situation of immediate adoption into a different family the environmental energies and those of the adoptive family that the focus will grow up in will be as instrumental as the genetic patterns of the birth parents, I imagine.

In addition to the family manifestation, the focus has to take into account the genetic codes of both the physical family lineage and the essence lineage: "You do not merely choose the parents that you wish to be manifesting through. You also are identifying with physical genetic codes which have been accepted within the established physically-focused family lineage. You also incorporate your own genetic codes, which are established throughout all of your focuses. Therefore, you may experience within a lifetime some element which may develop which seems to be outside of the genetic heritage of your family." (Session 174)

Body type seems to be part of the genetic focus coding; in that same session it is stated that the body type for the focus is often similar to that of other focuses of the same essence: "[…] you generally, not always but for the most part, choose to be manifesting within the same physical type. You may choose variations, but generally you manifest within this dimension of this physical focus with the same general type of body expression. You also carry the same type of genetic elements. This does not hold true entirely, for you may choose within any focus to deviate from this, and within extremes."

Even more decisions than the ones need to be taken, I notice in other sessions, namely those related to agreements with other essences; no focus comes into physical existence without agreements, it appears. Setting them up is also a part of the preparation process, but they are not cast in stone, as Elias points out in a.o. session 752: "You may change your expressions of agreement within any moment. I may express to you, you do not create expressions in which you engage in agreement with another essence to be creating any type of expression, and therefore it becomes an absolute. This is incorrect. You may express an agreement with another essence to potentially be creating a particular action or event together, but this is not to say that that agreement shall become an absolute, for you always hold the freedom of choice. Therefore, you may choose to alter the agreement or to disengage from an agreement."

Agreements may be made between two or more essences. They may concern relationships, of love or business or any other type. Some of them may be related to events concerning a few people, whereas others may involve thousands of people, such as war situations. The list is endless. I want to know from Lawrence if agreements are mostly set up to help each other. His answer is:

"These agreements you speak of, they are not always arranged for the purpose of helpfulness; they may be. There are many different purposes to these. It can be simply an exploration with the other individual in a different context. It may be for the purpose of jointly following similar intents. It may even be for the purpose of creating a family. It is very varied. And yes, helpfulness may also be an aspect of that. Generally speaking individuals do choose to project their focuses into time frames and locations together with others because of the past familiarity with those other individuals, and therefore the agreements make for different aspects of those relationships." (Private session)

Relationship explorations based on familiarity are the main triggers for shared focuses too, also between Lawrence and myself. Our explorations include much variety in relationship type:

> JANTINE: "I remember from our previous session that you and I have 600 shared focuses. Do you and I have a common theme in our shared focuses?"
>
> LAWRENCE: "It is not so much a theme. I would express that in this case it is simply a matter of familiarity and exploration of different relationships."
>
> JANTINE: "I assume there is lots of friendship between us in those shared focuses?"
>
> LAWRENCE: "Not always."
>
> JANTINE: "Right. Sometimes there are adversaries. It varies because we want to explore these different relationships."
>
> LAWRENCE: "Yes."
>
> *(Private session)*

I am quite sure that this is valid for my relationships with many or most other essences with whom I share more than one focus, and I even dare to say that that is true for the relationships between other essences too. Our individual intent is clearly not the only important feature in our lives, our relationships are equally valuable.

¶

The intent is set, the alignment, core truth, orientation, parents, locations, and all other elements are chosen, the agreements are made. On to the next step, the experience of the entering essence in the womb. Elias comments on this stage of preparation for the physical manifestation as follows in session 173: "[… although] you create this physical form from its inception, from the moment of its first cell, you within essence do not necessarily enter into the body consciousness at that moment. Each essence chooses at which point they are desiring to be entering into their design of their physical manifestation. Some essences may choose to be creating of a physical body consciousness, and not enter into this consciousness at all. In these cases, the physical manifestation does not continue. These may be looked upon within your view as miscarriages within your gestation, and also as aborted forms. This is not to say that these forms are not actual individuals, for they hold individual body consciousness. They only do not incorporate also the entirety of essence, for they have chosen to experience only partially. This, in differentiation to a focus which is born and continues, is an agreement equally between the entering essence and the parent; being obviously for the experience of both individuals, and often for many other individuals also which these experiences are affecting of."

Thus, a spontaneous or invoked abortion is agreed upon between the involved parties. If only the parents could accept that. It would considerably comfort them in their grief over the lost baby, especially in case of a miscarriage.

For me the situation has been straight-forward. The parents and sibling I have chosen as my family are very close to me in essence, with many shared focuses. I can say full-heartedly that we know each other well.

I have not made it easy for myself physically, by choosing a life-long metabolic disorder, but that has a purpose too, as Tompkin informs me in my first private session with him: "I would like to express that you chose this condition long before you arrived for it would help you actually look at the physical which is a part of your intent. And by focusing on the physical body it helps you solidify your exploration in your physical world. It also slows your energy down somewhat for innately you are a very fast moving essence. Your energy is very quick and light and you do tend to pass over things that may be important. [...] So this condition has kept you more cemented."

This piece of information on me having chosen the condition myself, and for a good purpose, is instrumental in enhancing my acceptance of it, and it widens my awareness as to how choice is key to my and everybody else's essence, before and during life. Now that I have covered pre-life decisions, I want to know what happens during life, and decide to dedicate my next investigations to that topic.

9

Me, my selves and I

I am in for a surprise when I start looking into the life of a focus in the Elias material. It turns out that each of us have innumerable aspects, or selves. I have multiple simultaneous lives going on, in multiple dimensions. In Elias' words, from session 133: "You hold many, many, many, underline, aspects of essence, more than you may count. There are intersections and interactions occurring continuously with you each from these aspects of essence. They may be alternate selves and their interactions [...]. They may be probable selves. They may be other aspects of energy within your essence, manifest for helpfulness within a specific situation. Your essence is focused upon you completely, as it is with all of its focuses."

Helpful, but I need more information to get a grip on this material, which I find in session 428: "I have expressed at times that you may view these different aspects of you in like manner to different emotions that you express. All of these different emotions that you identify are all you. They are all expressions of you and may not be separated from you, but they are all different expressions of you and are not necessarily primarily expressed simultaneously objectively. You do not express anger and joyfulness simultaneously objectively. You choose one or another. Therefore you create a primary expression in like manner to the primary aspect, which is your primary attention and direction of your focus."

So, I have alternate and probable selves as well as a primary aspect that I recognize as myself. But this primary aspect or self is not fixed. It changes positions, following session 362: "all of these you's exchange positions with each other, in a manner of speaking, therefore allowing many different types of expressions within one focus. Elements that may be dormant within one aspect of you may be quite expressed within another aspect, and in this, you may exchange what you may term to be "primary positions" of different aspects of self, and therefore alter your expressions. Now; in this action, at times you may be exchanging positions with another aspect that is expressive in a quite different manner than the expression of the primary aspect in which you hold familiarity. At these moments of the exchange of these types of aspects, there may be an objective disconnection with certain elements of memory, and the expression that is objectively projected may be quite noticeably different than the previous expression. This leads you, within your objective reasoning, to be lending energy to the idea and the belief of this concept of walk-ins, but in actuality, it is merely an exchange of different aspects of yourself, which are all expressed and are all present within each focus."

I am flabbergasted when I finish reading that snippet, and impressed by the potential effect of memory loss for the focus when a new primary aspect is expressing noticeably differently from the previous one. I suppose such change causes some confusion too, when familiar elements have disappeared. Not so strange that people consider such change of self a walk-in. In esoteric literature a walk-in refers to a more or less hostile take-over of a focus by another 'soul' (essence). Take-overs are not considered feasible by Elias, as he mentions in, amongst others, session 5: "This is a fantasy. Another essence will not be so rude as to invade your essence."

Temporary merges with other essences, your other focuses or your alternate selves do take place, he explains in session 147: "This is not to say that an exchange with another essence may not occur... obviously! (Laughter) Within agreement, an exchange may occur with another essence, but the body consciousness recognizes this exchange and is partially rejecting of this exchange. Physical elements occur, for the body consciousness realizes the essence occupying and directing ... We shall more express directing, for the essence does not float in and float out! But the body is recognizing of the direction and tone, which is different. Therefore, its response is to be rejecting of this. It will not reject alternates. It will not reject temporary exchange of other focuses of essence. It will be rejecting of another essence exchange."

I happily conclude that I will always be my multiple me, in all circumstances, also when changing primary position or merging temporarily.

¶

Now, what are those alternate and probable selves that Elias mentions as being aspects of essence? When I dive into the material to obtain an answer to that question I notice the existence of two more types of selves, the parallel self and the splinter. In addition, besides the physical reality also probable and parallel realities exist. As these probables are a huge topic, I decide to dedicate a separate chapter to them. I will limit myself in this section to providing a definition of these four types of self.

I feel relieved after making that decision. The material on selves is just too complex to be handled in one single chapter. Now I stand a better chance of understanding it more clearly.

Elias says the following about alternate selves in session 104: "Within essence, figuratively speaking now, you may view a focus individually being orbited by other aspects of each individual focus. These aspects are what you would view to be latent elements or qualities of the individual focus; you. As you travel through your sojourn of your focus, you draw from these orbiting elements, which are what you might perceive as alternate selves. These interact with you continuously, within consciousness. Within physical objective expression, they, at times, exchange places with you. They hold your vibrational tone quality. Therefore, there is an inter-exchange that may be accomplished."

Remember that I talked about the exchange of aspects, and the primary position in the section above? These aspects are all alternate selves. When a primary is replaced by another aspect, or alternate self, that previous primary becomes an alternate self.

Next in line is the probable self. I am already aware of its existence. During checks of dreams and out-of-body experiences Tompkin alerted me to this type of self, and I also searched for probable selves in two trips last year. However, I do not have much theoretical knowledge about them. I perform a search and find a workable description in session 1018: "In every moment that you generate a choice which creates a direction, you also generate countless probable selves. If you choose to be moving your physical location, at the moment that you generate that choice and move your physical location you also generate countless probable selves to be expressing all other probabilities in association with your one choice to move your physical location of your dwelling, so to speak. This is an example of how you generate probable selves. As you choose one mate, you also generate countless probable selves that choose other expressions."

While digging a bit deeper, I notice this snippet from session 309 that outlines the distinction between alternate and probable selves: "there is a definite difference between an alternate self and a probable self, for a probable self shall be creating of slightly different reality than you are creating yourself, whereas alternate selves shall be creating in harmony with you, for they are elements of you that occupy the same consciousness as yourself."

Clear enough. On to the parallel self. I like this workable description in a dialogue between Elias and an anonymous client in session 1479:

> ELIAS: "A parallel self can also be a probable self, but it would be a specific parallel. It would be a specific type of probable self that would be generated in a manner in which most of their experiences parallel your experiences. Or you may generate a probable self and YOU may become the parallel and you may parallel the probable. Or it may be not a probable self, it may be another aspect of yourself, an alternate you, which parallels your experiences."
>
> ANON: "Oh, interesting! This parallel would be another self or probable or alternate that... How can I say that? It will be parallel in my intent?"
>
> ELIAS: "Yes."

Understandable so far. What about the splinter? A splinter, Elias says, "would be a particular type of aspect of self. Splinters are those aspects of self which parallel you within a focus. As you manifest within a physical dimension, as I have stated, you hold countless you's. These are the aspects of you. Some of these aspects of you are quite parallel to you. [...] a splinter may be likened to the probable self in that it is a projection of you. The difference is that this particular type of projection may be projected into your officially accepted physical reality. You may meet another aspect of yourself that has been projected by you into this particular physical focus, and it shall be another individual holding its own integrity and creating its own choices within its own focus. It shall remain an element or an aspect of your essence unless it is choosing through its own desire to be fragmented and become its own essence." (Session 279)

In summary, a splinter is a focus of its own. I may even physically meet a splinter of myself in case I create one. A fascinating thought, but I think I would be very confused when bumping into a person who is also my essence and focus, but different from me nonetheless.

¶

From the information in the previous sections of this chapter it is clear that countless aspects of everyone of us exist in this physical reality as well as in parallel and probable realities. I want to find out a bit more about alternate selves, being the closest me's in my focus. I encounter a snippet in session 120 that further clarifies the notion of alternate selves. As the session was done with a person whose essence also belongs to the Sumafi family, the Seers, I can easily relate to this snippet:

"You may think of yourself as the television set. You are the television; this focus; but you may quite easily access any channel available within the frequencies that your individual set may 'pick up,' for there are some frequencies within your individual focus that you do not actually pick up within physical focus, for in your terms, they are far removed from you, occupying other realities quite removed; but within your pool of probabilities and your alternate selves, you may tune your consciousness to any of your individual channels, so to speak. Among these channels also is your Seer aspect; this being also, in your terms, an alternate self. This particular aspect parallels your focus continuously, and also intersects with the individual focus; the consciousness that you recognize. Each time, throughout your focus, or your 'lifetime' as you view it presently, that you are motivated to be seeking out truth and truthful, undistorted information, you are intersecting with the alternate self of Seer, which is an element or aspect of you. This element you may view to be similar to what you think of as your 'subconscious.' [...] Each time you are motivated to be investigating the undistorted information of any subject, it matters not, you are allowing a subjective intersection of the Seer aspect alternate self with your objective focus."

I could be intersecting with my alternate Seer self right now. An intriguing thought that I enjoy. My core truth of truthfulness must also be related to this alternate self, I suppose. My longing for least distorted information definitely. I appreciate that I have found that snippet. It makes the concept of alternate selves more tangible.

I wonder what happens in my dreams regarding these selves, and decide to launch a search on the topic. It doesn't take long before I find some interesting information in session 113: "[In dreams you] offer yourself the opportunity to view and interact with a conscious awareness, or what you view to be a conscious awareness; for you are continuously interacting and intersecting with alternate selves and alternate realities. You do this many times within your dream state, although you do this continuously regardless of your state of consciousness; but within your dream state, you allow yourselves, occasionally, to view the action. In this, you also offer yourselves the opportunity to be altering the action and changing the reality; (to Vicki) changing the color of the house."

So in our dreams we draw alternate selves to our objective consciousness, who, as us, show us alternate realities and actions that allow (and direct) us to make changes in our daily lives.

Before closing this chapter I want to find another example of accomplishing interactions with an alternate self, this time in waking consciousness. For my own and your comprehension. The following snippet, again from session 120, catches my attention as it is so easy to relate to the situation: "Let us view the scenario of choosing a new dwelling. You, intersecting with an alternate or probable self, are inspired to be moving into a new home. Within the process of seeking out a new home, you investigate many different dwellings. One may strike you as being what you view to be your perfect image of your dream house. In this, you have intersected, once again, with an alternate or probable self. Now; within the action of this intersection, you are creating the reality within the moment, but the reality also simultaneously already exists in what you view to be past, or future, or both; for within the reality of the alternate self, the existence is incorporated already. Therefore, as you step over your threshold into your prospective new home, you may feel a feeling of familiarity or comfort. Many individuals describe this as a "knowing" of this area. This house feels welcoming. The building of the house does not incorporate the feelings. It is not emanating emotion to you. The alternate self that you are interacting with and intersecting with is projecting emotion, feelings, and thoughts to you. You merge; therefore you feel the feelings. You do not always recognize these intersections, but they do occur. In this, the alternate self already occupies this house. The reality of this living space, and action of living within this space, is already existent, but it is not; for you are creating it within the moment!"

10
Probables

In the chapter on the creation of the focus I have inserted several Elias snippets that mention probabilities playing a part in the preparation phase of the new focus. The topic of all sorts of 'probables' has my undivided attention now. I start searching for a solid definition of probabilities in the Elias material and I find one in session 65: "A probability is a possible choice; therefore, there are countless numbers. You incorporate them singularly, one at a time. You choose one action. You choose from myriads of possibilities, which are probable choices. Each of the choices that you do not choose manifests elsewhere. All probabilities are actualized."

They appear to exist everywhere: "The subject of probabilities deals with experiences within all layers of consciousness. These experiences are parallel experiences. This may be viewed en masse or individually. All action within consciousness engages probabilities." (Session 111)

Probabilities are actualized in probable realities, which are created when big choices are made, it seems: "Probable realities are expressed in association with what you term to be significant choices, those choices that generate specific directions. Therefore, as you generate a direction and you continue in that particular direction, every moment and every choice within that direction is not generating a probable reality. But in the moment that you choose any particular direction in which you shall be generating movement, you do generate probable realities." (Session 1282)

Big choices are amongst others: getting married, obtaining a new job, having a child, starting a college study, or, as Elias uses as an example in the same session, a new business: "As an example, you generated a choice to be creating a business. In that moment in altering your direction, you also generated a probable self and a probable reality—in actuality several, but we shall focus upon merely one as an example. Now; in another probable reality, that individual did not engage the choice to be generating a business and continues to be employed by other individuals."

The distinguishing factor between creating other probable realities, and not creating them is a change of the direction you have followed until the moment of choice. A new friendship may well be in the line of your current direction, and will therefore not generate probable realities in which you do not start that friendship: "Now; you may be incorporating a friendship and not be generating a probable self or reality; it is dependent upon whether your direction changes." (Session 1357)

Now, where are they located, those probable realities? In parallel realities, it appears from session 481: "Alternate realities [where our alternate selves are located, red.] are a continuous action that are occurring involving all of the different aspects of you as this one focus, which all occupy this one dimensional reality. A probably reality holds a difference, for a probable reality and probable selves move into the position of what you may term as a parallel reality [which can be considered, red.] a type of parallel dimension in which you have created another you, which shall continue and shall be creating different choices from the choices that you view that you choose, but shall appear almost identical to you."

These probable realities are not far away from our daily reality. On the contrary, I would say; they seem to exist in a sub-dimension of our physical dimension: "a probable reality which occupies this same physical dimension, within a dimension of this dimension." (Session 313)

¶

Clearly our probable selves are located close by in consciousness, and seemingly large numbers of them are created at every significant choice as this snippet from session 279 states: "Now; be understanding that as you create a probable self scenario, you are not creating of merely one probable self. You are creating multiple probable selves that shall be experiencing all of the alternate choices that you have not chosen to actualize within the framework of this officially accepted reality."

What we don't do in this physical dimension, we do in probable others. That sounds very efficient to me. This way essence does not need to create other focuses to experience those other choices; they can all be worked out in the same life.

Worth mentioning is that probable selves lead their own life from the moment they are created and share their past with us, as mentioned in other session transcripts. In addition, they do not necessarily die when we do in physical reality: "All experience and all energy of all probable selves is available to all, but each is unique to themselves. Therefore, they continue within individual existence within their own value fulfillment; just as you are not absorbed back into the concept of essence as you disengage physical focus, for you are not separate. [...] The probable selves exist. They are all within the energy of you. Their motion, in a counter-to-parallel direction of you, occurs at moments of choice. They may follow your choice, or they may choose alternately. Each choice that you make affects all others, and each shall be influenced. Some shall actualize other choices. Some shall actualize the same choice with a different slant." (Session 152)

The statement that all our probable selves are in our

energy is another confirmation for me of the wideness of our being, and I just love to read it.

I am eager now to jump to my own experiences with probabilities and probable selves. I remember that this topic was touched upon in a session with Tompkin, as being related to my memory loss of childhood experiences. He provided me with the following information about my creation of probabilities: "You have actually created several probabilities as a child and you have actually jumped from one to another. And when this jump occurs you actually have a lack of memory that occurs for the experiences felt by one probability are not as strong as in another for you are not fully engaged in that probability […] You have jumped from one probability to another for you were wanting to be efficient once more and you were wanting to explore multiple probabilities all at once and you did accomplish this, however the end result of that is less retention of an actual physical memory." (Private session)

So, memory loss apparently is not limited to a significant change from a primary self to an alternate self with rather different preferences and traits. Juggling with probabilities has the same effect. Intriguing material.

Inspired by Tompkin's statement about my creation of probabilities I go searching for material on probables in my dream and out-of-body files. This dream apparently is taking place in a different reality:

> JANTINE: "[…] I have a couple of other dreams here. Ah, in one of them I kill a woman threatening to sue me and with a friend of mine we make sure she disappeared without a trace, under the floor. I have no remorse about the murder but some fear

for repercussions in 3D and other dimensions. And eventually she turns out to be still alive, the newspapers say. I am happy for that as the punishment will be less severe. Does that represent another focus of mine?"

Tompkin: "No, it actually represents an alternate reality somewhat in that you were exploring probabilities or outcomes. And solutions. And it was a very safe place to release frustration."

(Private session)

What a useful way to let go of some frustration. I laugh when re-reading this snippet, and appreciate the creativity of the human mind to release emotions safely in a dream, with no harm done to other individuals in physical reality. The fact that I feel no remorse in the dream about the murder was typical for that consciousness state too.

In that same session I check two out-of body trips with him that link to probabilities and a probable self (which I call parallel self):

Jantine: "[...] I have also been hunting for parallel selves. Only shortly and only in private consciousness trips. In one of them there was a little girl, 3 or 4 years old who paralleled, so who went into [another] reality, while my primary self made the choice to become more or less of a tomboy. Is that little girl indeed one of my parallel selves?"

Tompkin: "No, not quite. There was a probability explored at the time; however you decided to continue."

JANTINE: "OK, an exploration it was."

TOMPKIN: "Yes, it did not manifest necessarily into a separate parallel life. It was merely an exploration at the time."

[...]

JANTINE: "OK. Then there's an adolescent at 16 or 17 year old who paralleled after my primary self decided to bury down the sadness related to my father's death for a while.

TOMPKIN: "Yes, this one is correct."

JANTINE: "It became rather rebellious, and I, as primary self have never been rebellious."

TOMPKIN: "Yes, this is correct and you enjoyed yourself immensely." (Starts laughing; I follow suit)

JANTINE: "And that parallel self is still there or did it come back to me?"

TOMPKIN: "Still there, and still enjoying oneself."

I am happy that I have made the connection to these potential and actual probable selves. They have come to life not only subconsciously in a probable reality to which only my subjective awareness has access, but also consciously, in my objective reality. I must have countless other probable selves generated at other moments of important life choices, but I am not anxious to know about them at this stage. The above named selves serve their informative purpose for me and for this book. However, I have a short probable self related dream fragment that I want to share in this section, before closing this topic. It somehow illustrates the simultaneousness of the dream and 'actual' lives of my focus and probable selves. I brought it up for a check in a session with Lawrence last year:

> JANTINE: "My next question is also dream related, most questions are dream related. I was aware at one point within a dream that there was another dream, a parallel dream going on. Is it a correct conclusion to make that during the night lots of parallel dreams are going on?"
>
> LAWRENCE: "Your body consciousness, one body consciousness that you associate with you generally only engages with one dream at the time. However, your awareness that there are parallel dreams is an awareness of dreams that other probable selves of yours may be engaging in."
>
> JANTINE: "Right. That is really interesting! Would you say that I dream quite often of parallel selves? Where I just see them as myself?"
>
> LAWRENCE: "I would say that this aspect of you being aware of these parallel dreams is unique. It is not common."
>
> JANTINE: "OK. That is a fascinating thing. I do know that I have dreams in which I meet other focuses. Is it also true that I dream in my body consciousness of a parallel self, or is that never the case?"

LAWRENCE: "It occurs."

(Private session)

So, sometimes I am able to see a dream of a probable or parallel self, and sometimes I am such self in a dream. Fine with me. My curiosity about my selves in the physical dimension and in its subset of probable realities is satisfied for the moment. There are other dimensions to explore in which my essence operates. On to the next chapter.

11
Dimensions

As a former medium I have no doubt about the existence of other dimensions than our physical realm, nor about the possibilities to connect to them. My out-of-body experiences at the Monroe Institute and at home are of course also taking place outside our daily reality. So I have a working knowledge. From my investigations into free will after life I am aware that esoteric and religious literature has put other dimensions in vertical planes. We are supposed to work our way up on the ladder of enlightenment. However, as I already mentioned earlier in this book, Elias has stated that no hierarchy exists in and between consciousness realms or dimensions, which I highly prefer to the plane hierarchy. All consciousness is limitless and equal. It may be that many human beings lack awareness of that, but that doesn't change the wideness of their individual consciousness.

Parts of that consciousness are located in other dimensions, and I am eager to know more. Elias defines dimensions as follows in session 611: "Dimensions are merely areas of attention with consciousness; which means there are countless dimensions. They are not necessarily places. They are merely areas in which you direct your attention within consciousness, for consciousness IS all, and everything IS consciousness." Furthermore, "Let me express to you that dimensions do not hold numbers and they do not hold names. They are all sideways to each other. They are not higher or lower than any other. They are all simultaneous and they are all side-by-side." (Session 346)

Not only are dimensions sideways to each other, they also occupy the same space arrangements, Elias states in session 1556: "I may express to you as I have previously, all of consciousness occupies the same space arrangement. Therefore, as an example, within this very room that you are occupying in this moment, there are countless energies, literally countless, for within this space arrangement there are dimensions upon dimensions upon dimensions, and there are attentions upon attentions upon attentions, and essences upon essences upon essences superimposed in layers that are merely separated by perception."

'All' it takes to access other dimensions is a change of perception, it seems. Sometimes the access would happen unexpectedly, as mentioned in that same session: "At times, there is a slight crack in the layers, and at times there is an allowance of yourselves to glimpse briefly other expressions that occupy the same space arrangement. At times you may glimpse another essence, at times you may glimpse a manifestation of an essence. It may be a manifestation of your own essence; it may be a bleed-through; it may be an apparition. Apparitions are quite real. I have projected myself into them at times."

We may just bump into another focus of us, or into an energy projection of some other essence. Fascinating thought. We apparently have enormous amounts of other focuses in other dimensions, as mentioned by Elias in session 334: "Let me express to you that there are countless other dimensions, and there are many different focuses of essence that occupies each dimension. Therefore, it would also—in conjunction with the creation of the focuses of essence and the different qualities of different dimensions—be inaccurate to be stating any specific number of focuses held altogether within all of the different dimensions, for there is not in actuality a specific number of physical dimensions!"

Right. This matches his information in a private session, on the impossibility to provide a count of my other-dimensional focuses. Essences are literally everywhere. This dimension topic could easily become limitless itself, judging from the material that is available, but I don't aspire to obtain more theoretical knowledge about it. I determine to limit myself to the practice of accessing other dimensions and to the results of that practice.

¶

Visiting them on purpose is rather easy to achieve, it seems, although it isn't custom yet: "You may visit other dimensions to be accessing information of those other dimensions if you are so choosing, and you may also be accessing areas of consciousness that you view to be veiled presently. One area is that between yourselves and individuals that you view to be disengaged. You view a veil between yourself and those individuals. There shall be no longer this veil, and you shall allow yourselves interaction and communication, with the recognition of all of the aspects of the action of transition." (Session 339)

A word of caution though: when you project to another dimension, chances are that you contaminate their reality with your visit: "In your projection, you may experience what you assess as swimming with some of these fluid creatures. As you engage that action, you are merely exploring, and you are expressing curiosity and your own excitement in what you discover. In that reality, it translates quite differently and at times interrupts the configuration of manifestation of these fluid beings, and at times generates an action that within YOUR reality you would translate as a contamination of that fluid which appears to you to be water." (Session 1661)

I hope I haven't done that so far during my own visits. On the weekly out-of-body trips our focus hunt group has accessed many locations already. We mostly observe and seldom interact with the environment and its inhabitants in other dimensions than our own, in order to avoid such contamination. On one of our trips we went to the south coast of Portugal, bordering Spain, and wrote down our impressions afterwards, as always. I checked them with Elias last summer and it turned out that we had accessed another dimension during that trip:

> JANTINE: "[...] the three of us went for a hunt as whales and dolphins for a underwater city [trip] between Faro and Cadiz on the West Atlantic coast in the south of the Iberian island [...]. And we were discovering geometrical and soft line shaped cities and settlements. Is that something that you can relate to?"
>
> ELIAS: "Now what I would express to you in that is you are somewhat overlapping your focuses. I prospect you have connected with one focus which is here on earth in relation to the cetaceans and you are overlapping another focus which is other-dimensional and that is what you were noticing in relation to the shapes."
>
> JANTINE: (Somewhat confused) "By that you mean the shapes of the whales and dolphins?"
>
> ELIAS: "No, in the geometric shapes."
>
> JANTINE: "Oh! The geometric shapes point towards another dimension?"

ELIAS: "Yes, what you were doing was overlapping two different focuses in the same exploration, merely somewhat misunderstanding and thinking that they were the same focus but they are not."

(Private session)

So each of us met two focuses of our essences during that trip, one of the cetacean family, and one other-dimensional. We were flabbergasted and very content.

However, this isn't our only confirmed trip to another dimension; there are several. In one of them, which I brought up in a session with Tompkin, I went with Jan, one of my co-travelers, to another dimension, where a focus of mine was carrying out energy creation work:

JANTINE: "This is much fun. Another trip: as myself I went on a consciousness trip from the camel café and ended up in another dimension. The camel took me along as a kind of shamanic animal guide Two weeks later, with Jan, who has a very strong energy for this, we were together in another dimension and there I saw myself in a function of weaver of energy webs or energy fields, in that other dimension. Is that something that you can relate to?"

TOMPKIN: "Aha, my friend, I suggest you explore this one further for you have actually tapped into a relatively unknown area that has not been explored much by others. And when you share this experience with others, so that they may too explore this area and yes, you are somewhat of a weaver and what you actually do is take energy particles and weave them, as you were seeing, together to form items that you require. So you are actually seeing yourself creating items and generating what you wish. You were actually able to observe the process of that creation with a web."

(Private session)

I much enjoyed receiving that feedback at the time. Who wouldn't want to have a focus that was creating items out of an energy web? My ego was in a state of bliss.

Besides my weekly mind travels with our group I also participate in virtual dream events now and then. In one of those, led by a friend who is a dream explorer and lucid dream trainer, we set the intention to dream about dogs for three consecutive nights. The act of lending collective energy to this specific dog topic resulted in many dog-related dreams. I decide to dedicate an out-of-body trip to a dog dimension, and am quickly accompanied by several dogs when I have reached a relaxed trance state. The dogs and I indeed travel to another dimension, guided by Tompkin in dog disguise, he confirms in a private session:

> JANTINE: "[...] And last but not least I did a dream event with a couple of people into dogs. Our goal, our intention was to dream about dogs because I have been dreaming about dogs and I was invited to participate in the dream event. After we finished this, I much enjoyed doing this by the way, I went investigating by myself on a consciousness trip into the dog dimensions. Early on my way to these di-

mensions I received the company and guidance of about five dogs and further on a huge Great Dane came along as well, whom I had met on a previous trip, on a red planet. We went to a mixed human-dog dimension first, and then to a dog dimension with a human type of civilization. All inhabitants were dogs. I had a close bond with the Great Dane which really moved me. Did I indeed encounter a dog dimension or have I been very creative?"

TOMPKIN: "Hahaha! I ensure you, my friend, that I assisted you with this one for I was your guide dog so to speak and we did travel very far and it was to a different space and time as you accurately have interpreted. And yes, it is mostly filled with energy that is what you would view or picture as a dog. However, it is a similar energy consciousness or life form, but it is not a dog."

JANTINE: "I understand. It is a different kind of doggish energy."

TOMPKIN: "You project the image of a dog to make yourself feel more comfortable."

I, not a dog owner by the way, very much enjoyed the night and day traveling with dogs.

I want to end this chapter with another type of energy interactions stemming from outside our physical universe, one that appears in our peripheral vision. In the past half year there have been at least ten occasions in which I noticed a small bubble of light moving in the periphery of my right eye in my living room. When I turn my head, it is always gone within a second. I have been wondering if my right eye is experiencing some issues, but then I read a snippet on the Elias Facebook forum about the same phenomenon; from session 713:

> ANON: "The other thing that I can remember about this occasion is that in my peripheral vision, in the right eye, every time I turned my head there was a teal-colored diamond-shaped light or object that remained in this peripheral vision. Can you tell me what that was?"
>
> ELIAS: "You have pierced a veil of a dimension. You have allowed yourself momentarily to pierce through this dimension into another physical dimension. What you have viewed in your periphery is another aspect of you, that which may be termed as another focus of your essence, which occupies that physical dimension and not this physical dimension."

A focus of mine from another dimension entering my vision; this may be considered a bleed-through which, as Elias mentioned, is bound to take place much more often now that we are getting closer to the shift era of obtaining wider awareness globally: "All other universes occupy the same space; and once again I will express that it is not unusual, and you may look forward to viewing more and more imprints and bleed-throughs as you become closer to your shift. These are not expressions within your dimensional focus. They are bleed-throughs of other dimensional focuses, but you are viewing them now for your awareness is widening. I have expressed that this shift will be occurring globally. This has been an agreement which has been made in non-physical focus. Therefore it will occur, whether you are aware of its coming or not, and all individuals will be experiencing viewing the same occurrences whether they are physically aware of why or not." (Session 27)

An intriguing phenomenon, this shift. I have mentioned it here and there in previous chapters in the context of other topics, but now I put it on the main menu for the next chapter.

12
Shifting

In the chapter on essence I introduce the shift as a movement in consciousness leading to expanded awareness as well as to increased possibilities for conscious visits to other dimensions. While researching the topic more thoroughly, I quickly find out that there is a lot of information available, and I realize that it would take a book or two to describe the phenomenon in its entirety. My intention is to gain and then provide an overview of the shift, and although that will not be an easy task, I am determined to give it my best shot.

I estimate that the best approach is to start with the background of this consciousness movement. I launch a search query and start reading the transcripts. The first thing I discover is that the shift is an expression of a source event that originated in regional area two: "Every element of creation that incorporates mass events also incorporates a Source Event within regional area two, which is an agreement between many essences within collective consciousness. Your shift is a manifestation of a Source Event. The Source Event in itself is too great and expansive to manifest within any physical dimension or focus; therefore a facet, a fragment, an image of this Source Event will be translated into physical focus. The myth is much bigger than the expression." (Session 85)

Also, apparently it is not everywhere; it is limited to our dimension: "[…] this shift in consciousness is a mass event stemming from a source event which is connected to this physical dimension. It is not an action which is incorporated into all areas of consciousness. It is directly associated with this particular dimension." (Session 379)

The shift is ours. Reading on I notice that it started at the onset of the 20th century, and will last until approximately 2075. It contains various mass events, amongst which the two world wars. The source event of which the shift is a manifestation as well as a major mass event, which in itself consists of various mass events, includes Christianity: "Most of your Source Events are expressed throughout many, many, many centuries of your time. There are many mass events that are manifest as expressions of each Source Event. This allows for a diverse expression, within your physical focus, of many aspects of the Source Event; for as I have expressed previously, a Source Event may not be expressed into physical focus in entirety, for it is encompassing of much more than you may express within the limitations of physical focus, even spanning much of your time element. Therefore, you incorporate a tremendous time period to be expressing aspects of interpretations of your Source Events. This aspect, this expression that you have chosen to be now manifesting into your physical focus within the mass event of your shift, is another expression of one Source Event that also encompasses your religious focus."

While Christianity may be considered 'masculine', with one single male godly power figure and outward aggression, the shift tends to the traditionally 'feminine' symbol of the intuition: "Your religious expression is based in a manifestation, physically, with what you would attach to be a male orientation. You view God, within most of your religions within your globe, to be of male orientation, for this symbolizes, to you, power. […] within the beginnings of this shift, you are "swinging" to the female expression, realizing within your focus that you incorporate a necessity for valuing the intuitive self. You have allowed yourself an understanding that there are other elements of yourself, objective and subjective, that you do not view. You have learned, through your expression physically, that you are also more than the sum of your parts. Therefore, you hold a desire to experience more of yourself. As you move into the beginnings of your shift, you experience the quieter, more intuitive self. You allow yourself more of a connection with individual and also mass consciousness. [...] you may communicate, yes, you move into a more female-oriented area of consciousness in engaging this shift, although this is not to say that the females shall now be ruling your planet! [...] It now moves to the area of the male expressing, "I am needing to be more intuitive". (Session 100)

Males turning a bit more inward and connecting with their intuition; that sounds like good news to me.

¶

I am feeling more comfortable about the shift topic now that I know its background a little bit. However, I still don't know what the main reason is for its existence. I find out quickly; it turns out to be boredom: "You have all been practicing in creativity of imagination for thousands of your years. You have created tremendous belief systems to experience your ability in creating. Now, you have chosen to expand your focus. You have experienced all things possible for this physical focus in its present state. It is not necessary to continue repeating. Therefore, you choose a new experience. The new experience is to incorporate your essence and your consciousness into your physical focus. Even a child will become bored with playing the game too many times. You have been playing this game for thousands and thousands of your years. You are presently and globally bored with it. It is time to express yourselves in a new manner. You can only experience the same experiences so many times! It is not necessary anymore." (Session 13)

I am laughing out loud on my chair. So we needed a new game and in our collective consciousness we invented the shift to expanded awareness. It gets even better: in this new game negativity will have gone, I am reading in this snippet of session 18: "[…] this time of physical manifestation, incorporating negativity, is coming to its close. The game is almost over. However long you choose to continue playing is how long it will continue, although through agreement of all essences, in your future time as you view it, there will come a point of intersection where the game will end, whether you are ready for it to end, or not. As you experience and widen your awareness presently, you will become more in tune with yourselves. You will incorporate a greater understanding of your essence, and all of its probabilities, and all of its splinters, and all of its fragments, and all of its interaction."

Now that I know that, I want a more encompassing picture of this expansion, which I encounter in session 270: "This shift in consciousness is now, but in objective terminology shall be completed or entirely accomplished within the third quarter of your coming century. You have already moved beyond your midpoint within the action of this shift in consciousness, which was initiated in your physical time framework at the beginning of this particular century. Nearing the midpoint of your coming century, many elements shall be occurring that shall be definitive in turning your reality into an entirely new type of reality. That which you view as reality presently shall no longer exist. As to your physical forms, they shall continue as they are. As to your belief systems, you shall continue to hold belief systems, for these are a part of the design of this reality. As to the affectingness of these belief systems, they shall be rendered neutral. As to your physical societies, they shall be different. They shall be altered. Your approach to reality within this shift shall be altered dramatically, for your awareness shall be increased to the point of the inclusion of the remembrance of essence, which shall allow you greater freedom and mobility within this physical dimension."

I enjoy this prospect a lot! I wonder how this is playing out in our millennium, and continue my quest for information until I find this snippet in which Elias not only comments on current events but also mentions his contribution in helping out individuals by lessening the trauma during the shift: "You engage presently what I have designated in my terminology as a shift in consciousness, which is occurring presently and escalating and is affecting of all of you individually and also en masse. Odd and peculiar events occur within your present time framework, and this moves more intensely as you move forward within your linear time. In this, waves occur in consciousness. Let me express to you that there is no separation within consciousness, and although you view yourselves to be separate individuals, and within this reality objectively you are, you are also not. You are all interconnected within consciousness, and you hold no separation. You all hold affectingness to each other en masse and individually, and in this you share many experiences. Presently, within this now, a wave is occurring within consciousness which is directly involving this shift in consciousness. Many individuals are beginning now to be experiencing elements of trauma and confusion. Now; let me also express to you that as I have expressed many times previously, the reason that I speak with all of you is to be offering information in regard to this shift in consciousness, and in that to be affecting in lessening the trauma that shall be associated and IS associated with this shift. And now, it begins." (Session 284)

The trauma and confusion seem to be caused by hanging on to belief systems and not understanding the nature of our awareness such as our interconnectivity. Relaxing our beliefs is the key, not eliminating them as that is impossible due to the blueprint of our dimensions; belief systems are a key element in our blueprint, as you may remember from previous chapters. From session 99: "Within your individual expression presently, you experience conflict and confusion in widening belief systems. Within your shift, I do not use the term trauma lightly; for within your own experience, you already are becoming aware of the difficulty that is incorporated within widening in your awareness and recognizing belief systems, and also recognizing the reality of no right or wrong. You have existed for very much time within your present reality with these belief systems. Widening an awareness of these belief systems that you hold very tightly to creates conflict, for you do not willingly allow them to fly away! You have existed for much of your time period 'locked' into certain belief systems and accepted guidelines. It is as if you have 'rutted out' a pathway within a field. This pathway has been traveled back and forth continuously. Its scenery, its direction, its area has been accepted by you all, and has been used. Now, you choose to plow the entire field. You choose to widen, and allow yourselves the opportunity to experience all that lies beyond your small rutted path. In choosing this, you also incorporate trauma, for you hold very tightly to your accepted rut. You do not incorporate tremendous change very easily! You are beginning to view, individually, the difficulty in incorporating these changes of widening awareness. You are beginning to experience the confusion of letting go of accepted belief systems. Think now of the trauma that shall be incorporated, within a much larger scale of your entire globe!"

All this trauma he announces and describes in the snippets above in sessions that took place approximately 20 years ago, doesn't sound like much fun, but judging from the madness in current global affairs, in weather patterns and in frequent outrageous behaviors in humans, it seems quite accurate. The separation belief, which basically states that we are individuals with no inherent connection to others, each of us being an island, is one of the strongest beliefs we have, especially in the Western world. Letting go of this belief and being consciously aware of the interconnectivity between all people and all of consciousness will not be easy for most of us, me included. Meditating and writing down my dreams helps to feel connected to my essence, my own larger consciousness, I have noticed. The focus hunt sessions in which we mind-travel together have contributed a lot to feeling more connected with the group members and to get a sense of a general connectedness. However, I am aware I am not shifted yet in the spirit of the Elias definition, as I am still attached to 'us versus them' thinking patterns.

Luckily, Elias as well as other entities are helping us to lessen the trauma of the shift, as stated in the chapter on essence essentials, and now I remember that Tompkin mentions his supportive role in the shift in a private session of last year. While scrolling through my transcripts I find this snippet on his role: "I have my own intent and that is to assist people to explore what gives them joy and understand that the shift does not require a sense of depression or depriving themselves, it does not have to be difficult and if it is approached with more fun they will find their energy moves in a more efficient expansive manner so therefore I am attempting to assist people to recognize how to actually identify joy and laughter for some have even forgotten that."

This is uplifting information. It inspires me to move from a 'what I can't do yet' to a 'what I may well be able to do later' point of view. I start a search for more details on our current and upcoming abilities during and after the shift and it takes me just a few minutes on the Elias web site to encounter this snippet from session 72: "You are becoming more in tune to your own intuitive elements, your own inner senses, which effortlessly develop, and you notice. You experience viewing of other or unusual elements around you. Your vision becomes affected. You may view, visually, ordinary aspects of your lifetime, so to speak, differently. You may view, visually, elements that incorporate molecules and atoms breaking apart. In this way, you may see your table become "not so solid" and be wavy, for your outer senses are affected also within this widening. They become wider also, to incorporate a more realistic view and understanding of what you have created. Your hearing may become much more acute. Your touch becomes more sensitive. Your inner abilities are expressed through outer senses much more flowingly, without effort; this being why you will be viewing more individuals "tapping in," so to speak, to their psychic abilities or their hearing abilities. These are evidences of you moving toward your shift. You also become more aware of yourselves, and incorporate a fuller understanding of probabilities and their workings. As you widen, your understanding increases. These are all evidences of your shift."

I remember I had a conversation with Tompkin about how our group is moving through the shift together, and find this snippet in one of my transcripts on the usefulness of our trips in this shift era:

> JANTINE: "[...] With regards to what I do with the group and what we do in the group, in the group we are doing projections, we do remote viewing, we are learning objective stuff, we are discovering synchronicities, and that is all in the live 3D world. We are having lots of fun. We strengthen our ties. And what I am wondering, I do have the feeling that we are taking part in shift related and shift enhancing or speeding up activities when we are projecting. Is that correct? And if so, could you

elaborate on that, what we are doing subjectively while we are objectively projecting?"

Tompkin: "You are doing different things in each stage of what you described. With the projecting in particular you are somewhat assisting in an ease within the shift so that may appear to be lighter, easier."

Jantine: "Easier also for other people, we help also other people when we do that?"

Tompkin: "Yes, working within their own paradigms and belief systems."

Jantine: "Good. Thank you. Nice, because I did have that sense that we were doing more than just having fun exploring and discovering. So we are like let's say, facilitating an ease in that shift."

Tompkin: "Yes. Within their scope of belief systems. Some may allow more freedom and more ease than others."

Jantine: "That depends more or less on who we are touching."

Tompkin: "Yes."

Jantine: "And also I assume that some of us in the group are more involved with that than others. I can imagine that for example Debbie would be more into helping easing than I would as I am more exploration related."

TOMPKIN: "Yes. You each have your own roles, and each of your contributions are just as valid as the other. They are just somewhat different. But accomplishing all the same."

(Private session)

I am enjoying re-reading our contributions to the shift; they conclude this chapter. The next and last chapter of this book will be about transitioning, a process of preparation for the non-physical dimensions, in and after life. Lo and behold, also in that chapter the shift will be touched upon but mostly sideways.

13

Transition

While researching the shift I encountered the word 'transition' quite a bit. It seems to be a process related to both life and afterlife activities. I am still intrigued by life after death, even after writing an entire book about it, so I dive firmly and with lots of anticipated fun into the transcripted Elias material on this topic.

First I want to get a description of the phenomenon that will hopefully help me understand it. In session 116 I discover that it is nothing more nor less than the information process involved in moving one's individual awareness from one area of consciousness to another: "these individuals or focuses of essence are also experiencing and assimilating information; this being the definition of transition. You are moving within a transitional state from one area of consciousness into another area of consciousness, so to speak."

Transition activities take place from physical to non-physical and from non-physical to physical consciousness areas. The latter basically consists of an acclimation to the physical, Elias says in session 247: "There is an acclimation which is made into a physical dimension, for it is unfamiliar. Therefore, you allow yourselves a time framework to be acclimating yourselves into the reality of a physical dimension. Within this particular physical dimension, this may be moved into within six to twelve years. An individual may fully acclimate themselves into the official objective accepted reality as young as six years. At times, they may not be acclimating for twelve years, or any between."

I am actually more interested in the move from the physical to the non-physical. The information process in that move turns out to have many similarities to the shift objectives in that it is all about shedding belief systems and enlarging your awareness of your wider self. From that same session 247:

"Moving from physical focus into non-physical focus ALWAYS involves a transition, for you hold belief systems within physical focus and your attention is focused singularly in one area. Therefore, it is necessary for you to transition into non-physical focus [...], for non-physical focus does not hold belief systems and your attention is not singularly focused. Therefore, you may not move instantaneously from physical focus into non-physical focus without a transition period. This would be an action of explosion, so to speak, for your attention is singularly focused within any physical reality. Therefore, your attention only understands that reality. If moving instantaneously into non-physical simultaneous time, viewing all focuses and the vastness of essence, the focus would not comprehend. We are speaking of the focuses, not the entirety of essence! Therefore, the focus must be shedding the belief systems of the physical reality and widening its awareness and its attention to encompass all of essence. This may be accomplished partially within a physical focus."

If we wouldn't have such transition, we will go crazy, basically. We can choose to start transition in life as well: "Many individuals choose not to be engaging this action within physical focus, and in this they shall continue until the moment of their so-called death and then enter into the area of transition. Many individuals, though, ARE choosing to be engaging this action of transition while they are continuing within their physical focus. They may begin this action of transition at any moment. This is not to say that if they are engaging within the action of transition that they shall die, or that they are leading to their inevitable death! Although you are all leading to your inevitable death! (Laughter) But the action of transition is not the onset of your downward motion into the "depths of death." It is merely an action chosen to be addressing to your belief systems, expanding your awareness of your reality, re-engaging yourself with essence, and the action of remembrance while in physical focus; therefore allowing you less of a transitional state once you are entering non-physical."

Astonishing, the shiftiness of this transition process during life.

¶

As I have been rather busy tracing other focuses of my essences and peeping into other realities than our universe, I wonder if I have already started my transition. I ask a befriended forum member who is about to have a session with Elias if she is willing to ask him about that. My guess is that my transition started with or after my first program at the Monroe Institute in 2008. Elias confirms via my friend that my transition started in that same year. In a private session a month later I ask Tompkin in a private session if the program kick-started the transition, and whether my process is related to the shift:

> TOMPKIN: "The other way around. You started transition and thereby you allowed yourself more freedom."
>
> JANTINE: "Aha."
>
> TOMPKIN: "This was a communication to yourself that you are freer, you have increased abilities and it was an avenue to explore."

JANTINE: "So, already before participating in that program I had started transition and because of that transition I was able to do that program."

TOMPKIN: "Yes."

JANTINE: "Yes. OK. My other question related to this transition is: is it mostly related to me being able to handle the upcoming shift, is that why I transitioned, or is there another reason, like expansion in awareness before the shift? So, what would be the reason for me to transition?"

TOMPKIN: "A bit of both, related to your last question."

JANTINE: "So it does also help me get through the upcoming or present shift?"

TOMPKIN: "It is assisting you to have more awareness during the shift. You are already in it, my friend."

JANTINE: "Yeah, I know. Sorry, I used the wrong tense there. So it is helping me during the shift in increasing my awareness."

TOMPKIN: "Yes. And reducing trauma somewhat. And also allowing you further avenues of investigation."

(Private session)

Right! I am actively participating in my transition during the shift. I like that.

I continue to read about the transition process during life and notice that senility is another avenue to prepare for the non-physical consciousness areas after life:

"Within the action of transition within physical focus, you allow yourself remembrances. You allow yourself the opportunity to remember self and essence. You offer yourselves examples, viewings, actions—of consciousness, of essence, of more than your singular attention within an individual focus. You allow yourselves to reconnect with yourselves and the vastness of self. You may be choosing to engage this action for very few of your years within a time framework, or you may be engaging this action for very many of your years within your time framework. If you are accomplishing this within an expanded time framework, you shall confuse yourself less, for you slow your action. You allow yourself your time to be viewing singularly. You allow yourself your time framework to be viewing events one-by-one. If you are choosing to be engaging this action within a small time framework, you create your senility and you confuse yourself, for you enter simultaneous time. [...] If you are experiencing senility, the experiences are all happening at once and may not be excused away and you may be viewed as exhibiting lunacy, for you have become confused with your time element. [...] In actuality you are experiencing partial elements in preparation of simultaneous time within a particular focus, allowing you the preparation of moving into non-physical focus and not experiencing as much confusion initially." (Session 247)

Senility is a choice, like any other choice we make during life. It is clearly goal-oriented towards an easier process of transitioning after life, but not socially accepted in its expression of confusion during life.

9

Now that I know a bit about transitioning during life, I find myself ready to investigate into Elias' views on this process after we die. Apparently we do not start transition immediately after we die, in most cases. First we seem to enter a short phase of zero access to our objective awareness; a blink out time before we blink in to the non-physical after we disengage: "Now, understand this is an in-between period. [...] Therefore in your term and in your reality, it translates to approximately two weeks before the individual actually blinks in to the non-physical. [...] The body consciousness has disengaged but the individual's energy remains within your physical reality for approximately that amount of time. [...] There is no objective awareness with it. At all. In that blink, in the process of that blink, momentarily, in order to disconnect from the body consciousness the objective awareness in a manner of speaking, is turned off, temporarily. It turns on again once the individual blinks into the non-physical, temporarily." (Unpublished private session)

Step one after disengagement, the blink out. Then what happens? From session 1776: "Now; once that adjustment is implemented, the new experience may appear initially not to be new at all. What the individual moves into is the regeneration of the objective awareness, and therefore begins to create objective physical imagery once again. That imagery is associated with what is familiar, which is your physical reality. Therefore, the individual does not initially incorporate the memory of how they chose to disengage. In their perception, they have not disengaged. They continue to be expressing within physical focus and generating physical imagery and interactions with the individuals that they are familiar with. Initially, he shall not incorporate an awareness that you are not both continuing within physical focus. His perception shall be as it was before he disengaged, but there shall be some alterations, which eventually he shall begin to notice. The alterations of his reality shall be that there is less unpredictability, less surprise and moving into the point of no surprise. Also, the imagery that he generates shall appear to be more calm and what you would term to be pleasant, although he may not necessarily associate it with pleasant or pleasure, but neutral."

So, after the blink out-and-in, the individual creates a movie in which everything and everyone appears to be 'normally alive'. At some point, however, they notice a lack of surprise in the supposed communications, and they notice black holes. That leads to an expansion of their afterlife awareness:

"They begin to notice all of these holes that are in unusual places in their imagery and they begin investigating them. And as they approach each one they can feel a different energy being projected through that hole. [...] There is no image that they can see. They only see black. But they can feel the energy moving through it. And that prompts them to begin questioning more and more. [...] when they notice that their imagery immediately changes, merely from an intention—that their physical imagery changes—then they begin to experiment. [...] And in that, that is what generally leads them into remembering their death. [...] But it is not bothersome to them for they already see that they continue, that they are continuing imagery, that they can manipulate, that this is interesting, amusing, entertaining, fun and in that, they have already adjusted to nonphysical expression." (Unpublished session, March 2015)

I notice there is a different scenario for when the individual has very strong belief systems with regards to the afterlife, they may end up in for example a heaven or hell situation, until that movie breaks down, as mentioned in session 165: "You are a physically focused individual. You disengage physical focus.

You die. You, within this particular physical focus, hold deep religious belief systems; let us express Christian religious belief systems, for all of these individuals shall be familiar with these belief systems. Therefore, as you move into the area of transition at your death, you manifest these belief systems. You shall appear within your heaven. This shall be temporary, for this is a manifestation of your belief systems. It is what you expect. Therefore, temporarily you shall experience your creation of heaven. As you move into the action of transition, your heaven shall begin to dissipate, as a picture moving out of focus. It shall appear snowy and defocused. As this continues, you shall begin to lose your sense of time. As you lose your sense of time and you are losing your imagery you begin to feel . . . for you are continuing to objectively feel to this point . . . you begin to feel unsettled. This begins to unnerve you. At this point, other essences approach to be helpful. They provide stabilizing energy. This allows you to create imagery that you may understand as you move through transition. This is also helpful to you in acclimating yourself to simultaneous time."

I let this information sink in for a few minutes. I am glad that we will be able to notice deviations in our perception of reality, leading to an awareness of our death. I am also glad that we are helped by other essences once our belief systems and sense of time are breaking down. Especially when an individual has not participated in transition during their lifetime, the confusion must be overwhelming when their objective awareness falls away, as well as everything they ever believed in, including time.

I feel I need a break and decide to engage a short intermezzo related to communications with the disengaged. As you are probably well aware, about a thousand opinions and myths exist around such communications. Also Elias has expressed his views on this matter, I notice when reading through the transition information. He states that such communications often do not take place with the disengaged but with their energy deposits, that are created soon after disengagement; from session 296 : "Many individuals in the action of disengagement choose to be allowing energy deposits to be remaining within the area of Regional Area 1, physical focus. This is actual, physical, moving energy; that which you may term, in your language and in your terms solely, as living energy. It moves and it pulsates, and it holds elements of the personality of that particular individual which has occupied physical focus." Their function is, he says, is: "to be comforting at certain time periods to you, but the actual focus of the individual engages the action of transition, therefore is not engaged in direct interaction with individuals within physical focus, for individual focuses which are engaged in the action of transition non-physically do not interact directly with individuals within physical focus. In this, you may encounter individuals within physical focus that express to you that they are accessing a disengaged relative, so to speak, or friend, or any other individual. They are accessing energy which has been in conjunction with that individual focus, therefore holds its energy signature, so to speak, and also holds information of the individual, but is not the individual themselves, for the individual focus engages transition, and within the action of transition, that particular focus shall engage all of its attention in that area, viewing all of its focuses. Therefore, it does not directly interact with physical focus." (Session 339)

Interesting read. Mediums may, unaware, well be communicating with energy deposits while the disengaged individual is in transition; I may have engaged in such communications with deposits too in my medium years. I decide to ask Elias about that:

JANTINE: "Now, while studying the material of you, Elias, I also, of course, bumped into the communication from mediums with disengaged individuals or their energy deposits, and I was just wondering as I was participating in mediumship activities for a couple of years, what do you reckon? Was I more communicating with deposits or with disengaged individuals in transition? What was I doing at that time?"

ELIAS: "I would express that you were generating varying experiences. At times you were engaging other essences, at times you were engaging specific individuals that had disengaged and at times you were engaging energy deposits. In this I would say to you, if you think about it and if you allow yourself to genuinely assess it you would know it that what you experienced or what you felt was different at different times."

JANTINE: "Yes! And I totally agree and I have the sense that in the last part of the mediumship I had more contacts with deposits than with essences or disengaged individuals because it felt more superficial somehow."

ELIAS: "Ha! I would express that is considerably intuitive of you that you discerned that."

JANTINE: "So that intuition was correct."

ELIAS: "Yes."

(Private session)

I wonder how many practicing mediums will consider any of the information on communications with deposits. Their choice, of course. I re-direct my focus to my research on communications, and discover that when the disengaged individual is almost done transitioning, between brackets: you will find information about the actual transitioning process in the next section, they may choose to contact physically focused individuals. From session 116: "As you move through transition more completely (in your terms, these are your terms) while you continue within physical focus, you attain an awareness which is wider and may incorporate more conscious knowing action (also in your terms) within non-physical focus initially; for you eliminate moving through belief systems. This is not to say that these particular individuals do not move through belief systems presently. It is to say that enough awareness has been incorporated presently to be allowing of a manipulation of energy, in what you view to be a conscious action, to be connecting with physical focus in desire. [...] within this area of consciousness, non-physically focused, these individuals or focuses of essence are also experiencing and assimilating information; this being the definition of transition. You are moving within a transitional state from one area of consciousness into another area of consciousness, so to speak. Some essences choose to focus within this area of consciousness for what you would term to be great lengths of time; this being for the purpose of helpfulness to those individuals physically focused, offering information and validation of existence beyond physical focus, so to speak."

During the 'movie time' phase, when the individual is still creating objective imagery and has not noticed the black holes yet, such communications may occur as well, as this short dialogue in session 334 indicates:

KATIE: "Okay. Okay, I also had a visit with her, in a

meditation that I was in, the night after she died. Was this a connecting with her essence, or was this an energy deposit, or what was it?"

ELIAS: "This would be connecting not necessarily with an energy deposit, but with that particular energy of that particular focus disengaged, which occupies the area of consciousness that would be designated as between physical focus and the actual movement of the action of transition, for at times individuals do not move immediately into the action of transition but occupy a different area of consciousness first, for they are experiencing an objective type of disorientation initially upon disengagement."

A wide spectrum of communication possibilities, obviously. It may not be easy for a medium to distinguish whom or what type of energy they are contacting during a session, if they are willing to contemplate the specifications of their contact at all.

Back to the after life process. So, now the individual knows they are dead. They have the choice to enter transition immediately, but they can also opt to continue to play with objective imagery for a long or short while and enter the non-physical transition of shedding their beliefs and objective awareness at a later stage. The shedding of beliefs for a continuing focus is different from the action for a final focus, which is the last manifestation of an essence in their intended gathering of life experiences: "The individual experiences all of the viewings of all of the focuses simultaneously, but in choosing remanifestation, the belief systems held by all of the focuses are not addressed to. Only the belief systems that have been held within the individual focus are addressed to in this type of transitional state. Were this to be a final focus, the transitional action would be different, for all of the belief systems in relation to all of the focuses would be addressed to. This is an action of shedding belief systems and objective awareness, enabling the focus to move into non-physical areas of consciousness which do not hold belief systems or objective awareness." (Session 272)

In this transition phase the focus, continuing or final, notices their essence and all of their other focuses: "Once the individual begins to genuinely fully move into nonphysical transition, they begin to stop generating objective imagery. They begin to shed the objective awareness, and therefore also shed perception and move into a different type of expression. Once having assimilated the awareness of self as essence, of all the focuses of all of the different areas of consciousness and incorporating an awareness that they are an attention of this . . . [...] Once engaging that action and that awareness, there is much more of a freedom, for it is once again a matter of choice of how that attention shall express itself and in what direction. That attention may choose to be engaging another physical reality again. [...] Therefore, you may disengage, you may move through transition, and continuing as an attention, you may choose to be exploring another physical reality, or you may choose to be exploring other areas of consciousness that are not physical, or you may choose to be engaging in exploration of this physical reality in a different manner." (Session 1697)

What about skipping transition? Does that possibility exist? My question to Elias returns the following dialogue:

JANTINE: "Do disengaged focuses ever get to skip transition by their own free will or do all disengaged focuses go into transition?"

ELIAS: "Now, clarify that."

JANTINE: "Yes. What I am saying here is that I know that a focus, an essence always has free will and I know that there's the process of transitioning after disengagement at some point. What I was wondering is, is that transition something a focus is obliged to go through or can a focus decide 'no I am not going to do that, I am just going to stick with whatever belief I have now, or whatever I want to do'?"

ELIAS: "Ha! What I would say to you is, no, it is not obligatory. Therefore it is not obliged to engage in that transition but I would say to you that yes an individual could choose to remain in that stage in which they are continuing to generate objective imagery that mirrors physical focus, but generally speaking at different points the individual would become bored with that. They would move into that non-physical transition because that is the action that sheds the objective awareness and the belief system of that particular reality. And that allows that individual to move in any other direction that they choose. If they choose not to engage that transition then they are choosing to remain in that stage and continue to be in that stage and eventually that would become limiting."

(Private session)

One gets bored, eventually, hanging around in pre-transition areas. I ask Elias if the boredom that led to the Shift is related to focuses not shedding their beliefs after disengagement. Apparently there isn't, but a link does seem to exist between overcoming limitations in transition and in the Shift:

> ELIAS: "[...] In this point you have explored your reality from a particular perspective and that has been somewhat exhausted and it has becoming limiting, therefore the point with this shift in consciousness is to allow you to expand your objective awareness much more and therefore give you much more freedom in what you explore and what you create. The more self aware you are, the more freedom you have to explore and to create in different capacities. You are shedding the limitations that you have to this point, not the beliefs."

> JANTINE: "Thank you for that! That is clarifying. [...] I was wondering like maybe we are doing a lousy job after life and that creates so much repetition in similar kind of experiences that we became bored. But that is not true. No."

> ELIAS: "No. This shift in consciousness is entirely about your freedom and your experiences and your creations in physical focus."

> JANTINE: "Yes. And [the boredom that led to the Shift has, red.] has nothing to do with hanging on to beliefs that have not been examined."

> ELIAS: "No."

(Private session)

When transition is over, the aware and subjectively focused individual continues its existence the way they choose: "At that point they choose whether they want to engage in other physical realities or explore other areas of consciousness non-physical. They have many, many choices." (Unpublished session, August 2013)

One of these choices, obviously, is providing information in the sense that Elias does, and Bashar, Abraham, Kris, as well as Seth in the last century, as well as many more essences.

The focus has reached the non-physical again, after its creation many chapters ago. Time to embark on new adventures.

Not yet for me, though! I have places to go, people to meet, and lots of earthly fun ahead of me before I am out of here.

Afterword

What a ride! Loved every bit of the research, the writing and the chats with the ghosts. I hope you have enjoyed the read.

Based on the material I have presented in the book I can only conclude that the wideness of our being is immense; it is endless. We are consciousness and we are present everywhere, in all consciousness areas and dimensions including our own, with its 3D, parallel, probable and alternate realities.

If you are interested to know more about the various topics I have introduced in the chapters, check out the Elias web site. You will find that there is much more material on these topics available there, as well as on many other topics that I have not touched upon as they do not fit into the scope of this book.

Actually I think that each chapter topic and each other topic in the Elias material deserve their own book, and I hope that someday these books will indeed be written.

References

The Elias session numbers in the book refer to published session transcripts. The quoted excerpts of these numbered transcripts can be accessed on the Elias Web site at *www.eliasweb.org*.

The copyright for all Elias sessions lies with Mary Ennis, as mentioned on the Elias web site at the above named address. My private sessions with Elias are not available on that web site in any format, nor are the transcripts of the unpublished sessions that I have used excerpts of.

The copyright for all Tompkin sessions lies with Tara Shaw, as mentioned on the web site at the below named address. The transcripts of my sessions with Tompkin are partly available at *www.tompkin.info*.

The copyright for all Lawrence sessions lies with Nuno Romao. The transcripts of my sessions with Lawrence are not available publicly. Furthermore, there is no web site with Lawrence material currently existing on the internet.

About the Author

Jantine Brinkman is the author of *Free Will after Life* and an investigator into a wide range of consciousness phenomena.

www.ingramcontent.com/pod-product-compliance
Lightning Source LLC
Chambersburg PA
CBHW030911080526
44589CB00010B/245